Best w

John Travo

Lynton and Lynmouth

Glimpses of the Past

Lynton and Lynmouth
Glimpses of the Past

JOHN TRAVIS

The Breedon Books
Publishing Company
Derby

First published in Great Britain by
The Breedon Books Publishing Company Limited
Breedon House, 44 Friar Gate, Derby, DE1 1DA.
1997

ISBN 1 85983 086 2

Printed and bound by Butler & Tanner Ltd., Selwood Printing
Works, Caxton Road, Frome, Somerset.

Colour separations by RPS, Leicester.

Jackets printed by Lawrence-Allen, Weston-super-Mare, Avon.

Contents

Acknowledgements 6

About this Book 7

Early Visitors 8

The Valley of Rocks 14

Accommodation for Visitors 20

Roads to Lynton 24

Sea-fishing 29

Smuggling 32

The Lynton Revel .35

Holiday Pleasures .38

Stagecoaches 49

Paddle-steamers 59

A New Curate Arrives 65

Royal Visits 68

Floods 73

Lynmouth Coastal Traders 79

Sea Rescues 87

Elevating the Masses: The Cliff Railway 93

Progress? 99

Sam Colwill: Coachman 112

Hollerday House .119

Cutting the First Sod 131

Developments at Woody Bay 135

Day-trippers 152

The Coming of the Motor Coach 158

The Lynrock Mineral-Water Company 168

The First Months of War 173

A German Bomber 179

Index 187

Acknowledgements

I am very grateful to the many local people who provided information and assistance while I was preparing this book. Special thanks must go to Wally Gilson and Harriet Bridle for loaning me so much useful material.

Particular mention should be made of the help so generously given me by the staff at many libraries and record offices. I owe a particular debt to Joy Slocombe, Curator of Ilfracombe Museum, and Les Franklin, Librarian of the North Devon Athenaeum, both of whom gave me invaluable assistance.

While working on this book, I was fortunate to have a surprise caller. Jim Dillon, a New Zealander, provided me with some fascinating material about his uncle, a Spitfire pilot who in 1940 helped to shoot down a German bomber over Martinhoe Common. Warm thanks are due to him and to Flo Hildick, who gave me her memories of the incident.

I am extremely grateful to Andrew Farmer who read my draft and rescued me from some of my errors. He also gave me invaluable assistance in dating my illustrations.

I should like to thank John Loveless, of Lyndale Photographic, for processing my photographs so expertly, and Bill Pryor for his sterling work with the photocopier.

As always, I owe a big debt to Gwyneth, my wife, who provided so much practical assistance and encouragement.

Lastly, I would like to thank Justin, Emma, Sarah, Ruth and Simon, my children, for reading my manuscript and making some constructive suggestions for its improvement. This book is dedicated to them.

Illustration Acknowledgements

Special thanks are due to the following people and institutions for granting permission to reproduce illustrations in this book:

Bath Hotel: 73; Harriet Bridle: 43, 67 (left); Paddy Coles and Molly Friend: 174; Devon and Exeter Institution: 9, 12, 17 (top), 26 (bottom), 49; Jim Dillon: 179, 181, 182 (top), 182 (bottom), 184, 186; William Durman: 50 (top right), 128, 177; Andrew Farmer: 17 (bottom), 22 (top), 24, 26 (top), 29, 31 (top), 37, 38 (bottom), 40, 44, 58, 68, 75, 83, 87, 90; Wally Gilson: cover (back top), 39, 45, 84, 94 (top), 100, 132, 169; Paul Gower: 33, 57 (top), 63, 124; Ann Hobbs: 46 (left), 110 (top); Ilfracombe Museum: 15, 21, 22 (bottom), 23, 27, 41 (bottom), 50 (left), 51, 54 (top), 60, 69, 70, 72, 81, 94 (bottom), 95, 97, 102, 105 (top), 105 (bottom), 112, 113, 114, 115, 116, 117, 118, 131, 161; Betty Jaques: 14, 25, 31 (bottom), 38 (top left), 67 (right), 76 (top), 77 (top), 77 (bottom), 79, 80, 89, 93, 99, 107 (top), 153; Edna Jewell: 133, 162; Lyn and Exmoor Museum: 127; Lyndale Photographic: cover (back bottom), 38 (top right), 42, 47, 48, 52, 57 (bottom), 82, 85, 88, 103, 104, 109, 121, 136 (top), 136 (bottom), 143 (top), 143 (bottom), 144, 146, 148 (bottom), 154, 155, 158, 160, 164, 166, 170, 175; Lyndale Photographic (courtesy of Lyn and Exmoor Museum): 137, 138 (top), 138 (bottom), 147 (top), 147 (bottom), 150 (top), 150 (bottom), 151; Lynton and Lynmouth Town Council: cover (front), 10; Ernie Norman: 54 (bottom), 165 (top); North Devon Athenaeum: 168; John Oldham: 135, 139, 140, 141 (top), 141 (bottom), 142, 145, 148 (top); Bill and Eileen Pryor: 46 (top right), 46 (bottom right), 50 (bottom right), 53, 107 (bottom), 122, 123, 130, 134, 165 (bottom), 171; Andrew Richards: 35, 76 (bottom), 106, 110 (bottom), 119, 152, 163 (top), 167, 176; Mike Simpkins: 56, 163 (bottom); John Travis: 11, 32, 41 (top), 55, 62, 71, 125, 126.

About this Book

This book sets out to recapture the flavour of life in Lynton and Lynmouth in earlier times. The written word is provided by residents and visitors who were eyewitnesses to both important events and everyday happenings. When necessary, brief explanations accompany the passages. Prints and photographs have been included to illuminate the text.

This is a book which had its beginnings in the research I did for my *Rise of the Devon Seaside Resorts, 1750-1900* (1993) and my *Illustrated History of Lynton and Lynmouth, 1770-1914* (1995). After publishing these two histories I found that the shelves of my study still bulged with files of unused information. While browsing it occurred to me that I had more than enough colourful material to form the basis of an interesting anthology. My main difficulty was in deciding which passages to include and which to leave out. The focus of attention was to be Lynton and Lynmouth, but I decided to cover a few events in neighbouring parishes when happenings there seemed to be of particular relevance to Lyntonians.

The first tourists arrived in the twin villages in the late eighteenth century, and in the years that followed the holiday industry gradually replaced farming and fishing as the main economic activity. This book does not attempt to chronicle these changes. Instead it provides a series of glimpses of life in the twin villages at various times in the past.

Finally, a few points to help the reader. Original spellings have been retained, so some place-names appear in a variety of forms. Locals will notice that some of the street, hotel and restaurant names are not the ones we know today. Some of the passages have been abbreviated and omissions are indicated by three dots. At the end of each item its source is given, so those who find their appetite whetted can track down the original publication and enjoy reading the full version. Please read on; I hope you enjoy the book.

Early Visitors

IT WAS IN THE 1790s that the first tourists began to arrive in Lynton and Lynmouth. In earlier times most travellers had avoided the barren wastes of Exmoor, but now they began to make the difficult journey over the moors, lured by reports of the unusual landforms to be found in the Valley of Rocks.

Amongst these early visitors were some poets. The new Romantic Movement drew its inspiration from the world of nature, so its leading spirits felt trapped in the crowded towns and longed to roam free in unspoilt countryside. These young poets were delighted when they reached Lynton and Lynmouth for the scenery exceeded all expectations.

Samuel Taylor Coleridge

Samuel Taylor Coleridge several times made long journeys to see Lynton and Lynmouth. In 1797 he and William Wordsworth were living in the Quantocks in Somerset, and in November they walked 30 miles along the Bristol Channel coast to visit the twin villages. It was on this expedition that Coleridge planned the *Ancient Mariner*. In the following year he repeated the walk, this time taking William Hazlitt with him. Hazlitt later wrote an account of their visit to Lynton:

> We had a long day's march — (our feet kept time to the echoes of Coleridge's tongue) — through Minehead and by the Blue Anchor, and on to Linton, which we did not reach till near midnight, and where we had some difficulty in making a lodgment. We however knocked the people of the house up at last, and we were repaid for our apprehensions and fatigue by some excellent rashers of fried bacon and eggs.
>
> The view in coming along had been splendid. We walked for miles and miles on dark brown heaths overlooking the Channel, with the Welsh hills beyond, and at times descended into little sheltered valleys close by the seaside, with a smuggler's face scowling by us, and then had to ascend conical hills with a path winding up through a coppice to a barren top,

Lynmouth in 1810. The picturesque village had been attracting visitors for some 20 years.

like a monk's shaven crown, from one of which I pointed out to Coleridge's notice the bare masts of a vessel on the very edge of the horizon and within the red-orbed disk of the setting sun, like his own spectre-ship in the *Ancient Mariner*.

At Linton the character of the sea-coast becomes more marked and rugged. There is a place called the Valley of Rocks bedded among precipices overhanging the sea, with rocky caverns beneath, into which the waves dash, and where the sea-gull for ever wheels its screaming flight. On the tops of these are huge stones thrown transverse, as if an earthquake had tossed them there, and behind these is a fretwork of perpendicular rocks, something like the Giant's Causeway.

A thunderstorm came on while we were at the inn, and Coleridge was running out bare-headed to enjoy the commotion of the elements in the Valley of Rocks, but as if in spite, the clouds only muttered a few angry words, and let fall a few refreshing drops. Coleridge told me that he and Wordsworth were to have made this place the scene of a prose-tale, which was to have been in the manner of, but far superior to, the *Death of Abel*, but they had relinquished the idea.

In the morning of the second day, we breakfasted luxuriously in an old-fashioned parlour on tea, toast, eggs and honey, in the very sight of the bee-hives from which it had been taken, and a garden full of thyme and wild flowers that had produced it…

We returned on the third morning, and Coleridge remarked the silent cottage-smoke curling up the valleys where, a few evenings ago, we had seen the lights gleaming through the dark.

William Hazlitt, 'My First Acquaintance with Poets', The Liberal (1823)

Lynmouth, c.1813. Fishermen's cottages line Mars Hill.

Robert Southey

In August 1799 Robert Southey travelled along the Exmoor coast from Minehead to Ilfracombe. He was greatly impressed with Lynmouth:

> My walk to Ilfracombe led me through Lynmouth, the finest spot, except Cintra and the Arrabida, that I ever saw. Two rivers join at Lynmouth. You probably know the hill streams of Devonshire: each of these flows down a coombe, rolling down over huge stones like a long waterfall; immediately at their junction they enter the sea, and the rivers and the sea make but one sound of uproar. Of these coombes the one is richly wooded, the other runs between two high, bare, stony hills. From the hill between the two is a prospect most magnificent; on either hand, the coombes and the river before the little village. The beautiful little village, which, I am assured by one who is familiar with Switzerland, resembles a Swiss village, — this alone would constitute a view beautiful enough to repay the weariness of a long journey; but to complete it, there is the blue and boundless sea.

C.C.Southey, Life and Correspondence of Robert Southey (1849-50), Vol. 2

Lynton, c.1840. The old farming village lies in a sheltered hollow below the church. Most of the newer houses and hotels have sea views.

Percy Bysshe Shelley

In 1812 Percy Bysshe Shelley took his young wife, Harriet, to spend the summer at Lynmouth. Shelley wrote:

> This place is beautiful… Mountains certainly of not less perpendicular elevation than a thousand feet are broken abruptly into valleys of indescribable fertility and grandeur. The climate is so mild that myrtles of an immense size twine up our cottage, and roses blow in the open air in winter. In addition to these is the sea, which dashes against a rocky and caverned shore, presenting an ever-changing view. All shows of sky and earth, of sea and valley are here.
>
> Edward Dowden, The Life of Percy Bysshe Shelley (1886)

While at Lynmouth Shelley was inspired to write his celebrated *Queen Mab*, but at the same time he was also penning revolutionary tracts. With the nation locked in battle with the French in the Napoleonic Wars, it was the height of folly to write

Lynmouth in 1829. By this time a few large houses had been built for wealthy incomers or to accommodate visitors.

anti-Government literature, but Shelley was not a conventional man. Dreaming of a new political order, he thought up some eccentric ways of distributing his tracts, launching some into the sea and sending others into the sky attached to small hot-air balloons:

> We discover Shelley — a boyish figure — in the August days, alone… on the Lynmouth beach, pushing certain small boxes, each with its mast and sail, from the rocks; or watching from his boat a little flotilla of dark green bottles, tightly corked, which rise and sink as the waves sway them seawards. Or we see him in the twilight launching his fiery craft, laden with truth and virtue, into the evening air. On returning to the myrtle-embowered cottage from such adventures as these, Shelley would speed his envoys on with the breath of good wishes winged by song.
>
> Edward Dowden, The Life of Percy Bysshe Shelley (1886)

The Valley of Rocks

LOST IN WONDER, early tourists entered the Valley of Rocks. Here at last was the steep-sided vale they had travelled so far to see. They seemed determined not to be disappointed! Their accounts convey a feeling of awe mixed with curiosity. Imagination ran riot as they tried to find explanations for this deep cleft in the hills and its remarkable rock formations.

A Wonder of the West

Here are Robert Southey's impressions of the Valley of Rocks in 1799:

> The Valley of Stones, a spot which, as one of the greatest wonders in the West of England, would attract many visitors if the roads were passable by carriages. Imagine a narrow vale between two ridges of hills somewhat steep: the southern hill turfed; the vale which runs from east to west, covered with huge stones and fragments of stones among the fern that fills it; the northern ridge completely bare, excoriated of all turf and all soil, the very bones and skeleton of the earth; rock reclining upon rock, stone piled upon stone, a huge and terrific mass. A palace of the Preadamite kings, a city of the Anakim, must have appeared so shapeless, and yet so like the ruins of what had been shaped after the waters of the flood subsided.

Valley of Rocks, 1762. This early print shows the valley before it began to attract tourists.

> I ascended with some toil the highest point; two large stones inclining

on each other formed a rude portal on the summit: here I sat down; a little level platform, about two yards long, lay before me, and then the eye immediately fell upon the sea, far, very far below. I never felt the sublimity of solitude before.

C.C.Southey, Life and Correspondence of Robert Southey (1849-50), Vol. 2

Prehistoric Circles and Human Sacrifices

How delighted the early tourists were when they came across groups of standing stones in the Valley of Rocks. Here was something they were keen to investigate and account for. In 1789 John Swete, a South Devon gentleman, had no doubt these stone circles were Druid in origin:

Several circles, huge masses of stone, in diameter above forty feet, I observed in the central part of the Valley, which seem to have been appropriated to the uses of the Druids, either civil or religious! — a spot

Valley of Rocks, c.1828. The group of large stones beneath Castle Rock are the remains of a stone circle.

so peculiarly adapted to those mysteries, which were to be kept inviolate and conceal'd from the profane intrusive eye.

Devon Record Office, 564/M, John Swete, 'Picturesque Sketches of Devon', Vol. 1

Some early visitors thought it likely that prehistoric man had used the Valley of Rocks as a natural amphitheatre in which to perform human sacrifices and other cruel rituals:

To the admirer of Druidism, the Valley of Stones must present a high gratification, when considered as the scene of the ancient rites, the secret superstitions and barbarous immolations of that remarkable order. The retired situation, the awful appearance of the impending rocks, and the wild romantic character of the place, peculiarly mark it as a spot devoted to their sanguinary religion.

T.H.Williams, Picturesque Excursions in Devonshire and Cornwall (1804)

The Threat of Enclosure

By the 1790s the Valley of Rocks was becoming an important tourist attraction, so it was hardly surprising local people were incensed when the lord of the manor proposed throwing up walls to make part of the Valley of Rocks his private domain. In 1796 John Swete made a second visit to Lynton and in his journal expressed horror that anyone could consider marring the valley's wild grandeur:

A few years ago the Manor of Linton, of which this extraordinary valley forms part, was purchased from a gentleman of Exeter for the sum of £1300, or thereabouts, by the Mr Lock whose neat house I have noticed at Linmouth... The neighbourhood had to regret that the Manor had changed hands, for the possessor now residing on the spot, seem'd to exact from the leasehold tenants more than he might in justice claim, or they be induced to cede. The Valley, in particular... which was a commonage to many of the contiguous farms, he had requested might be yielded to him for a warren, to the intent, such was the current rumour, that having got it on such a view into his possession, he might afterwards arrogate it to himself and throw it into cultivation. In this scheme the

Valley of Rocks, c.1840. The valley was common land so local farmers could graze their animals.

Valley of Rocks, c.1830. A desolate scene, but visitors admired the grandeur.

proprietor was disappointed, happily so for the public, for in the distraction which agricultural inclosures would have made from the wildness of the scene, there would have been in a picturesque light so much lost.

Devon Record Office, 564/M, John Swete, 'Picturesque Sketches of Devon', Vol. XII

The lord of the manor had suffered a rebuff, but only a temporary one, for by 1801 he had succeeded in erecting a wall round part of the valley floor. In that year T.H.Williams, an artist, visited the valley and expressed outrage at the damage done to the natural landscape:

On entering the Valley of Stones the eye is offended by a quadrangular wall built with the small stones which lie scattered about; having been lately erected, not a single blade of grass rises on it, to break its natural deformity and relieve the sight from so disgusting an object.

T.H.Williams, Picturesque Excursions in Devonshire and Cornwall (1804)

Removal of the Standing Stones

In 1854 there was another enclosure dispute involving the Valley of Rocks. It was between Charles Bailey, owner of the Lee Abbey estate just to the west of Lynton, and the Roe family, lords of the manor of Lynton. Charles Bailey published an open letter in which he claimed he had no intention of walling off part of the Valley of Rocks. He accused the manor authorities of damaging the valley's scenic beauty and claimed they had taken away the standing stones:

Many misrepresentations have been made and industriously circulated, to impress you with a belief that I am seeking to destroy the romantic and beautiful scenery of the Valley of Rocks... These impressions were made, doubtlessly, for the purpose of improperly continuing the dominance of those who have misused it for the last fifty years, and have committed and encouraged the commission of multitudes of act; such as the building of ugly stone walls and fences, the removal of the immense Druidical stones and circles, and the rocks which formed its peculiar and striking interest and beauty, for the purpose of selling them for gateposts.

Devon Record Office, 52/14/2/6, The Division of the Lynton Commons

Those who walk the country round Lynton today may look at the large gateposts guarding the entrances to fields and wonder if they might once have had a much more important status as part of a stone circle. The stones cannot be returned, but at least we have good cause to be grateful that the Valley of Rocks remains an open area of outstanding natural beauty.

The stone wall controversially erected at the beginning of the last century by the lord of the manor remains, but time has mellowed it. Perceptions change; now the wall is considered such an attractive feature that some years ago the Council had it restored.

Accommodation
for Visitors

WHEN the first tourists arrived at Lynton and Lynmouth in the late eighteenth century they found a lack of suitable accommodation. The twin villages were humble places and had no hotels.

A Request

In 1789 John Swete wrote in his journal:

> There is a little public house at Linton called the Crown, where, though the accommodations are but indifferent, the people are civil and attentive. It cannot but be an object of request that a better inn and even lodging houses were built on the plain at Linmouth for, as the beach is very tolerable for bathing… if the roads for a few miles were made more passable, which at little expense might be effected, I know no place more likely to be resorted to during the summer months, for none in Great Britain I think can exceed it in the beauty and magnificence of its environs.
>
> Devon Record Office, 564/M, John Swete, 'Picturesque Sketches of Devon', Vol. 1

The First Tourist Accommodation

The first proper tourist accommodation was provided by a Lynton man. William Litson was one of the dealers who had previously made a living buying wool from Exmoor farmers, employing locals to spin it in their houses, and then taking the finished yarn to Barnstaple to sell it to the weavers. In the 1790s increasing competition from mechanised mills in other parts of the country led to the collapse of the local spinning industry and he was obliged to look for new business opportunities. In his 1853 guidebook Thomas Cooper, a Lynton doctor, described how William Litson came to open the Valley of Rocks Hotel:

Amongst these dealers was the late Mr William Litson who in the beginning of the present century was thus driven to seek some other employment. Finding from time to time strangers wending their way to  the spot on account of the unique and picturesque scenery, he opened in 1800 what is now the Globe Inn as an hotel, and furnished the adjoining cottages for the accommodation of visitors. Amongst the first of these was the late Mr Coutts the banker, and the Marchioness

Lynmouth, c.1828. The tall, white house had recently been built to accommodate visitors.

of Bute. The scenery becoming known, the visitors soon increased; this induced Mr Litson to build the Valley of Rocks Hotel, which he opened in 1807.

T.H.Cooper, A Guide Containing a Short Historical Sketch of Lynton and Lynmouth (1853)

Romantic Views and Choice Wines

In June 1808 William Litson placed an advertisement for his new hotel in an Exeter newspaper:

VALLEY OF ROCKS INN AND TAVERN, LINTON, DEVON. William Litson returns his grateful thanks to the nobility, gentry, and public in general, for the great support he has received the past seven years, and respectfully informs them, for their better accommodation, he has at a considerable expense erected a large and convenient house, in a desirable

The Valley of Rocks Hotel, c.1830. It had been opened in 1807.

situation, commanding most delightful and romantic sea and land prospects, which he has furnished with good beds and every other requisite, and has lain in a stock of choice wines and liquors; with these advantages, united to good stabling, and coach houses, and an unremitted

Lynmouth from the valley of the East Lyn, c.1840. The house on the cliff between Lynmouth and Lynton is Clooneavin, a gentleman's residence.

Lynmouth, c.1835. On the left, beyond the bridge, is the New Inn. This little tavern was in existence by 1778, before tourists began to arrive.

attention, he presumes to solicit a continuance of their favours, which will ever be acknowledged with unfeigned gratitude.

Families accommodated with board and lodging, and all the comforts of a private hotel.

Linton is most delightfully situated... not above half a mile from Lymouth, a sea-port in the Bristol Channel, and commands a most extensive view of the south coast of Wales, the Holmes, Lundy island, and other grand and picturesque scenery; at a short distance from the stupendous Valley of Rocks, and various cataracts, and in an excellent country for hunting, shooting, or fishing; there is also a beautiful beach, and fine clear water for bathing.

Exeter Flying Post, 2 June 1808

In the years that followed other hotels and lodging-houses were opened. The twin villages were being transformed into a small coastal resort catering for a wealthy clientele.

Roads to Lynton

EARLY TRAVELLERS were a hardy breed! At the end of the eighteenth century there were no proper roads to Lynton and Lynmouth for carriages to run on, so tourists had to walk there, or go on horseback, finding their way along ancient trackways over the moors. These difficulties did not deter them.

A Difficult Descent

The following description of the trackway down Countisbury Hill was written in 1799 by Richard Warner, a Bath clergyman, who had walked from Minehead. He saw danger in every step:

> The small church of Contisbury, perched upon a hill, indicated that I was about three miles from Lymouth, and here my guide of the preceding day had informed me that I was to expect "a nation strange road". In truth, he had not excited my curiosity in vain, for perhaps this public way may be considered as one of the greatest wonders of North-Devonshire. Narrow, rugged and uneven, it creeps along the face of a prodigious rocky down, that runs with a most rapid descent to the ocean, which is roaring below, at the depth of five or six hundred feet. Formidable as the precipice is, the neigh-bouring inhabitants have not

Lynmouth from North Walk, 1865. By this time there was a proper road down Countisbury Hill. It can be seen in the distance on the left.

> so much as erected a low wall, or stretched a friendly rail along its brink, to lend their aid in case of accident or darkness; so that should the traveller's horse become restive whilst treading this perilous path, or he

himself mistake the way, nothing could probably prevent his immediate destruction. But this road, so alarming to the stranger, is totally divested of anything like horror to the Devonian. Custom, which reconciles all that is fearful or disagreeable, painful or terrible to the mind, enables him to travel it with perfect indifference, and whilst I was descending the most abrupt part with the greatest caution, a Devonshire peasant, seated upon a laden horse, and driving three others before him, passed by me down the declivity at the rate of a dashing postillion upon a good turnpike-road.

Revd Richard Warner, A Walk through Some of the Western Counties of England (1800)

The First Roads

By 1820 work had begun to make Lynton and Lynmouth more accessible by land. John Lock, the lord of the manor, began the work of constructing roads. William

The road into Lynton, 1853. It had been made about 1813.

Sanford, the wealthy proprietor of Nynehead Court in Somerset, further improved the access after deciding to have a summer residence, the Lynton Cottage, built at Lynton. An 1825 guidebook informed visitors:

The road to Watersmeet in 1865. It had been made in 1837.

A few years ago this place was known only as a fishing creek: the roads to it were impassable even for carts, and the only place of public accommodation was a miserable ale house. By the indefatigable exertions of the landed proprietor, Mr Lock, new lines of road were opened both here and in the immediate vicinity. Carriages then began, though with difficulty, to find their way and a small inn was established. The place became more attractive to strangers and gained the particular attention of W.A.Sanford Esq., who promoted the beneficent designs of Mr Lock by causing the roads to be widened and improved.

Guide to All the Watering and Sea-Bathing Places (1825)

Castle Hotel, Lynton, c.1850. Some visitors arrived in private carriages, so the hotels provided stables and coach houses.

To Lynton by Private Carriage

Once roads had been constructed a few wealthy tourists began to travel to Lynton

The two-arched bridge over the East Lyn at Lynmouth in 1854. In 1860 a larger, single-arched bridge was built to replace it.

and Lynmouth from distant parts of England in private carriages. They would hire fresh post horses at each posting inn along the route. In 1823 Mrs Selwyn, a lady who was touring the country, journeyed by carriage from Ilfracombe. Her comments suggest that the road was atrocious and that there were no posting inns along the way where the horses could be changed:

> The drive from Ilfracombe to Linton is through the worst of roads, it exceeded all we had met with. I believe it is but seldom used as we did not meet with a turnpike. In our way to Linton, the stage being twenty miles and the horses fatigued, the drivers gave them beer; two large jugs divided among the four.
>
> Mrs Selwyn, Journal of Excursions (1824).

Meeting Carriages

It became usual for Lynton hotels to keep post boys ready with extra horses to go out to meet the private carriages and help drag them into the village. Fights would break out as these hotel employees tried to secure custom for their establishment. In 1833 the new tenant of the Castle Hotel placed an advertisement in the *North Devon Journal* complaining at the way the Valley of Rocks Hotel tried to attract trade:

> Castle Hotel, Linton: The present occupier flatters himself the accommodation cannot be excelled, and he also begs to notice that the practice of one of the other inns, in keeping persons constantly on the roads watching for carriages, with a variety of fabrications to induce families to go to the Valley of Rocks Inn, is entirely below the respectability of the above establishment.
>
> North Devon Journal, 19 August 1833

Looking for Customers

The fierce rivalry continued and in 1851 one guidebook found it necessary to warn intending visitors that the Lynton hotels had telescopes trained on the top of Countisbury Hill looking for private carriages approaching.

> At Lynton, telescopes are employed at the rival hotels for the prompt discovery of the approaching traveller. He had better, therefore, determine beforehand on his inn, or he will become a bone of contention to a triad of post boys, who wait with additional horses at the bottom of the hill to drag the carriage to its destination.
>
> Murray's Handbook for Travellers in Devon and Cornwall (1851)

Sea-Fishing

FOR centuries Lynmouth had a thriving fishing industry. Enormous shoals of herring appeared in the Bristol Channel each autumn. Vast quantities were caught.

The Herrings Disappear

The following account describes the mysterious disappearance of these shoals at the end of the eighteenth century:

Lynmouth originally was a small village consisting entirely of huts and drying houses, the inhabitants depending on the curing of herrings. The shoals of these fish then frequenting the shore from the beginning of September to the end of October were occasionally so abundant that tons of them were thrown away or used as manure. Indeed the peasantry

Lynmouth, c.1825.

ascribe the desertion of the coast (in 1797) to the insult offered to the fish by using them as manure on the field, whereon now stands the house of Mr Roe at East Lynmouth...

The period from 1787 to 1797 was the last occasion, after an absence of exactly 40 years, of the herring being caught here in sufficient quantities annually to form a trade; they were chiefly sent to Bristol for export to the West India Islands. During these ten years from September to the end of October, the sea at Lynmouth was literally one mass of herrings...

With the exception of one abundant shoal in 1823, and one previously on Christmas Day, 1811, when the inhabitants were called out of church to take them out of the weirs, they have not been caught in any quantity since 1797. Whether the clergyman joined in the rush from the church to the shore, report sayeth not.

T.H.Cooper, A Guide Containing a Short Historical Sketch of Lynton and Lynmouth (1853)

In the second half of the nineteenth century there were still occasional years when enough herring were caught to warrant some being salted down for the winter. The days of plenty, however, had gone for ever and only a handful of men made their living by fishing.

The Fishermen Stay

Yet old sea dogs still congregated around the harbour each day, took occasional boat trips and chatted to tourists. In 1877 one visitor poked gentle fun at one of these 'seafarers':

About Lynmouth beach are lots of 'fishermen' — none of whom ever fish, at any rate, for a livelihood; but who do boating jobs, put passengers aboard the steamers, and generally potter about for a living in connection with the sea. One of them, surnamed by his comrades 'the Ancient Mariner', is quite a character. To hear him talk of his sea-experiences, and his knowledge of everything connected with the craft, from the duties of a quarter-master up to those of Admiral of the fleet, and to listen to his disquisitions on foreign seas and the precautions which would have saved

The quay at Lynmouth, 1864. The figures near the Rhenish Tower are probably visitors, those on the quay may well be boatmen.

every ship which has been wrecked within human memory, one would suppose he had sailed round the world some scores of times, and knew every nook and corner in its four quarters — whereas, truth to tell, his world is bounded by a circle described by a bee-line carried twenty miles out from Lynmouth as a centre, and the Bristol Channel is the only 'ocean' with which he is even partially acquainted.

North Devon Herald, 11 October 1877 ·

Lynmouth, c.1880. By this time very few boats were engaged in commercial fishing, but cargo vessels still used the harbour.

Smuggling

MENTION the word 'smuggling' and most people conjure up romantic pictures of lanterns flashing far out at sea, of barrels of brandy being run up in moonlit bays, and of brave men defying callous customs officers. There is some truth in all these images, but it is only fair to point out that smugglers were determined law-breakers who would stop at nothing when challenged.

Folk tales abound of smuggling on the lonely coasts near Lynmouth. Yet it is difficult to find hard evidence of these nocturnal activities. Newspapers only carried accounts when the gentlemen of the night were arrested.

In 1832 a group of smugglers were caught red-handed at Lynmouth. This

Lynmouth, c.1836. In 1832 a gang of smugglers had been surprised by coastguards while trying to run contraband ashore here.

Lynton, c.1880. The coastguard's house can be seen above the highest terrace on the left. Built in the mid-19th century, it commanded a fine view of the coast.

resulted in the Barnstaple-based *North Devon Journal* carrying a remarkable story about a remote coastal village, which never normally made the news:

> On Saturday last, a vessel was seen to go up channel off Ilfracombe, and lay to for the tide a short distance from Lynmouth. On being hailed, she said she was laden with china clay, and bound for Gloster: but from some suspicious circumstances, she was watched by the men on the preventive service; and in the night a boat came to shore laden with upwards of thirty kegs of brandy, which a number of farmers were assembled to take off on horses.
>
> The preventive men, three in number, seized the spirits and three horses, on one of which one of the men mounted and rode off for Porlock, to procure further assistance. In the meantime another boat

laden with spirits came to the spot, and the crew immediately commenced an attack on the officers, and severely beat them; during the scuffle the two horses were rescued, and the smugglers subsequently returned to the vessel with their boats leaving the officers in possession of sixty-four kegs of spirit.

The vessel immediately set sail and put in near Appledore, where she landed the remainder of her cargo, and then proceeded to sea. She is reported to be a pleasure yacht, the property of a gentleman of Appledore. Of the portion of the cargo that had been landed at Appledore, 22 kegs were seized by officers of the customs on the spot, and 16 others which had been conveyed by a boat up the river and lodged on the premises of a person in the parish of Heanton, called Bedford, whose house is situate on the strand, fell into the hands of the excise officers of this town.

North Devon Journal, 26 January 1832

A Lynmouth coastguard subsequently arrested two local farm labourers at Countisbury on suspicion of having been involved in the incident. These men were later convicted of smuggling, but their fines were immediately paid. Was it the Appledore shipowner who found the money in order to buy their silence? We shall never know.

The Lynton Revel

THE LYNTON REVEL was the principal festival of the year. Held at Midsummer it was a time of music, merriment, feasting and drinking. The highlight was always a wrestling tournament. In 1912 Andrew Richards, a Lynmouth man well into his eighties, reminisced to a *North Devon Journal* reporter about the revel in the 1840s:

The event of the year in the olden days was Lynton Revel, a day on which the twin villages were *en fete*. The revel was held annually on the 24th of June. An announcement of the proceedings was couched in the following terms: 'Lynton Revel, June 24th. Six large silver spoons; these to be wrestled for. Six teaspoons to be skittled for at Dan Lashbrook's Globe Hotel. Spoons to be worn in the hat on Sunday by Nathaniel Vellacott, the champion wrestler, so that every person might see what is going to be given.' According to the custom the spoons were worn to church, attached to a hat, which in shape was something like a cockade. The teaspoons were worn by a man of the name of Richard Vellacott of Lyn.

A large crowd would

Andrew Richards, c.1912.

assemble at the Globe Hotel to witness the wrestling. The wrestling, however, was somewhat different to that known to the present generation. The competitors used to kick one another until one was almost exhausted and offered little or no resistance. A ring was formed and the combatants were decorated by red and black caps which they respectively wore. To the ringmasters was allotted the task of keeping the crowd back with large sticks, and if anyone encroached upon the ring they invariably felt the stick across their shoulders. The spoons were worn by the man who threw his opponent three times, 'three fair backs' being the term used. A band was engaged for these occasions consisting of William Bale (who was afflicted with blindness), from Kentisbury, and a man named Peake from Combe Martin, the former playing the violin and the latter the 'bass viol'. Mr Smith, with his shooting range, was a well-known character at Lynton Revel, with his 'Penny a shot and 40 nuts every time you win'. The late Mr Thornby (Barnstaple) and Jennie Morris (Combe Martin) provided the inevitable nuts, gingerbreads and comfits.

North Devon Herald, 7 March 1912

Later in the same year the *North Devon Journal* published the memories of Mr W. Hooper, another octogenarian, about the Lynton Revel in the 1840s. This account serves to remind us that Devon wrestling was a brutal sport, with contests usually continuing until one man's shins were bleeding so badly that he was unable to continue. Mr Hooper remembered an amusing incident:

A feature of the wrestling was the effective use that was made of the legs. A really good wrestler had to be a really good kicker, and he had himself to have legs as tough as iron.

I remember on one occasion one resourceful wrestler tried to guard his legs in an unusual way. He was a young man from Challacombe, and for the sake of comfort he padded his legs.

He seemed quite unconscious of the most vicious kicks, much to his opponent's surprise. The explanation, however, was soon forthcoming, for in response to a particularly brilliant effort on the part of his opponent, the bottom of one of his trouser legs split, the stuffing fell out,

St Mary's Church, Lynton, 1865. In earlier years the silver spoons which were to be prizes in the wrestling matches were exhibited here before the revel started.

and the luckless young fellow fled amid the laughter of the delighted crowd.

North Devon Journal, 11 July 1912

In his 1853 guidebook Dr Cooper included a description of the Lynton Revel. His account was written only a few years before the festivities were discontinued. The revel was coming under fierce attack from moral reformers, who argued that the wrestling was barbaric and was accompanied by heavy drinking:

Lynton Revel begins on the first Sunday after Midsummer Day. It formerly lasted a week. A barrel of beer was placed near the church gate in readiness for the people coming out of church, who partook of a glass and a cake, called Revel Cake, made with dark flour, currants and caraway seeds. Wrestling formed a chief feature in the amusements, and large sums were raised by subscription to purchase prizes. However odd it may appear, it is not more than twenty years since, that the silver spoons bought as prizes to be wrestled for, were exhibited hung in front of the gallery in Countisbury Church during divine service on Revel Sunday. Of late years, however, owing to the prevalence of drunkenness, especially on the Sunday afternoon, the respectable inhabitants have set their faces against these revels, which have now dwindled into insignificance. The collusion which sprang up among the wrestlers to share the prizes without them being won by a real trial of skill and strength, hastened also greatly to abate the enthusiasm of the subscribers, so that years of late the prizes have not been beyond a few shillings on the ground. This of itself has given a death-blow to the Revel.

T.H.Cooper, A Guide Containing a Short Historical Sketch of Lynton and Lynmouth (1853)

Holiday Pleasures

St Mary's Church, c.1882. Many visitors attended Sunday services. The church has since been altered with a major extension being completed in 1904.

Outside the Royal Castle Hotel, c.1920. Visitors enjoyed exploring the area on horseback.

Watersmeet, 1865. This beauty spot attracted many visitors.

NINETEENTH-CENTURY visitors to Lynton and Lynmouth were generally moneyed people who came for long stays, so they had both money and time to spend on a wide range of recreations.

Shooting Seabirds

A lady visiting Lynton in 1830 found herself involved in a shooting expedition:

It was proposed to take an excursion on the water, for the purpose of surveying the cliffs along the coast, towards the Valley of Rocks; and also that one of our party might have an opportunity of shooting some of the sea birds which frequent those crags in great numbers and varieties; cormorants, murrs, parrot-bills, naths, sea-pidgeons, gulls &c. &c.

A boat being engaged at Lynmouth, we left at one o'clock, and were

Lynmouth in Edwardian times. Visitors congregate by the river.

soon below the enormous precipices of the 'Old Man' and 'the Castle', appellations bestowed on the two most prominent cliffs adjoining the Valley of Rocks. Unfortunately for us, a thick mist hung over the upper portion of the crags, obscuring their summits from view, and at times descending even to the water's edge.

After rowing some time among the rocks that here throng thickly about the shore, the wild screaming of the birds announced that we had disturbed them from their accustomed haunts. Several young, yet unable to fly, sat in the crannies of the rocks, others rose on the wing, and flying off to the sea, afforded a mark to the shotsman; the old ones all the time soaring beyond reach, and screaming in wild rage at this invasion of their peculiar domain. The echoes from the cliffs, prolonging the report of the shots, perhaps contributed to their alarm, though we were informed by the boatsmen that they are often visited in this way by sportsmen, and

The cliffs west of Lynton, c.1830. Many sea birds nested here.

also, that in the season, it is usual to search the ledges of the crags for eggs, of which a large quantity is sometimes obtained. One of these men had frequently, he said, climbed the cliff on this perilous employment, an adventure, to judge from the appearance of the rocks, of no small risk.

S.Dixon, A Journal of Eighteen Days Excursion (1830)

Student Pranks

Students often visited the twin villages in the summer months. Some of these young men ran riot, but, because they had money to spend, their behaviour was tolerated. In 1912 an elderly resident reminisced about their behaviour half a century earlier:

> Lynmouth in those days was not without its influx of summer visitors, and was made the yearly rendezvous of a party of gay young college students. They were perfect terrors, and it was a matter for conjecture as to what joke they would be perpetrating next. On one occasion they unhung the Manor gates and put them across the old Lyndale Bridge, and they also loaded the guns in the Manor field and fired them off in the dead of night. The old summerhouse on the hill was precipitated over the cliff. Another of the favourite jokes of these young collegians was to screw up every door in the village so that it was only by forcing the door that it could be opened in the morning. Farmer Nicholas Jones lost a number of his ducks and offered a reward for information which would lead to the discovery of the perpetrators of the theft. Two days later the ducks were

View of Lynton and Lynmouth from the summer-house on Summerhouse Hill, in the early 1830s.

The summer-house, c.1850.

discovered in a bathing machine near the beach. The above is but a sample of the jokes which were played by these young students.

North Devon Herald, 11 April 1912

Sea-Bathing

Bathing in the sea was an important part of the holiday ritual. At Lynmouth, as at most seaside resorts, the sexes bathed separately, ladies and girls just to the west of the harbour, men and boys from the remote beaches at Sillery Sands and Wringcliff Bay.

Bathing machines on the west beach, mid 1860s.

Ladies wishing to bathe had to use a bathing machine. In reality little more than a hut on wheels, it was introduced in order to protect their modesty while changing, and to allow them to be transported into the sea, safe from prying eyes. Imagine the bumpy ride as the machine was trundled over Lynmouth's rocky foreshore!

By the 1850s males were being encouraged to actually swim in the sea, rather than just to dip themselves in the water, but for most women bathing was still an unpleasant ordeal rather than a pleasure. Female bathing attendants supervised every movement the ladies made, and still sometimes carried out the traditional practice of dipping them under the waves in the belief that the sea water had therapeutic properties.

In his 1853 guidebook, Dr Cooper describes the sea-bathing at Lynmouth, but fails to adequately explain that all males wishing to bathe would first have to face a long walk:

> A machine for bathing in the sea, was a few years since built by subscription, and is entrusted to the bathing women for the use of visitors, the surplus profits being devoted to the keeping of the machine in repair. About half-tide is the best period for bathing in the machine. Independent of this, many persons are in the habit of proceeding along the shore towards the Foreland, as the tide is receding, where there is a beach, only to be reached at low water, adapted for the purpose. There is also a little bay well suited for bathing at high water or half-tide, called Wringcliffe Bay, immediately under the Castle Rock in the Valley of Rocks, to be reached by a path just beyond this rock.
>
> T.H.Cooper, A Guide Containing a Short Historical Sketch of Lynton and Lynmouth (1853)

Fern Collecting

The Victorians were insatiable collectors. Rare birds were stuffed to be displayed under glass domes, anemones were plucked out of rock pools to be exhibited in home aquaria, and rare ferns were ripped out of Devon combes to be replanted in domestic ferneries.

The following extract comes from *Fern World*, a book published in 1877. Sadly, Francis Heath, the author, failed to realise that publicising the rich

FERNS !
FERNS !
FERNS !

FERNS from Devonshire, Cornwall, and Somerset. Instruction Book for making Rockery, planting Ferns, &c., with each 5s. order. 14 named varieties. 6s. per 100, parcel post; 30 good plants, 2s. 6d. Two Choice FILMY FERNS (Hymenophyllum, Tunbridgense, and Unilatarale) 2s. per foot, free.
1000 varieties, British and Exotic Ferns. Sycopodium, &c. Fern Spores (Seeds), British and Exotic. Best varieties, true to name, 12 packets 2s.; 26, 4s.; and how to grow them. Catalogues post-free, 2d. Established 28 years.
The Fernery is open daily for Visitors, where choice varieties of Ferns can be seen, collected in Devon, Cornwall and Somerset, during the last 30 years.
GILL'S BOARD & LODGING HOUSE, Victoria Fernery, Lynton, North Devon.

Advertisement for the Victorian Fernery, c.1885. The proprietor collected wild ferns to sell at his shop.

Glen Lyn, 1853.

profusion of ferns growing near Lynton and Lynmouth would inevitably cause many fern collectors to make the resort a place of pilgrimage, with the result that the stocks of the rarer plants would be greatly depleted:

> Entering Lynmouth, the central point of attraction for the lover of ferns is Glen Lyn, the whole of which is enclosed and in private hands… The Lyn roars down its steep and rugged glen to the sea in a succession of the most beautiful falls over huge mossy boulders, studded with marvellously developed forms of fern life. Now as we follow down this enchanting valley, there is a sudden dip in the course of the river, and the rapid onflow of the current precipitates its waters in one great volume into the channel below. Now, as passing under the shelter of over-arching trees, we come upon a spot where the river bed falls more gently in its course, the flow of the current, less rapid, becomes more musical, and we look in wonder upon a fairy, dreamy scene of clustering ferny forms in fascinating association with mossy rocks and flowing water.
>
> Francis Heath, The Fern World (1877)

Monsters from the Deep

At the beginning of the twentieth century visitors to Lynmouth could go on deep-sea fishing trips with every chance of returning with quite remarkable hauls. These trips were led by Cecil Bevan, a man with an amazing gift. Living in an age when monster fish still lurked in the deep waters off the North Devon coast, he knew just where to find them.

Cecil Bevan was a hotelier by trade. In fact he had grown up in the business, for his father was William Bevan, the proprietor of both the Lyndale and Tors Hotels. In 1895 William Bevan had extended his Lynmouth empire by opening the Lyn Valley Hotel, and Cecil had been made the manager.

The Lyn Valley Hotel in the Edwardian era.

Cecil Bevan in the Kingfisher, *c.1905.*

Cecil Bevan's record catch, weighing 675lbs., December 1908.

John Totterdell, bell-boy at the Lyn Valley Hotel, c.1902.

Blessed with a pleasant beaming face, a sunny temperament and a strong Devon accent, Cecil soon became a real favourite with his hotel guests. Yet often he left hotel duties to his wife and staff, for fishing was for him a consuming passion. He lived for the hour when the incoming tide made it possible to head out into the Bristol Channel in his boat, the *Kingfisher*.

Quite often Cecil Bevan reckoned his haul in hundredweights. On 1 December 1908 he set a record for a catch off Lynmouth which is unlikely to be beaten. Weighing 675lbs., it included 35 conger, two skate, four cod fish and a pollock.

The following account was written by a journalist who accompanied Cecil Bevan on a sea-fishing expedition in the autumn of 1901:

> Having heard of certain great conger, resembling dragons, and skate of prodigious size being caught at Lynmouth, and finding myself at liberty, I accepted the kind invitation of Mr Cecil Bevan to join in his sport with what is locally called a 'spiller' and, according to the arrangement, found

Quite a catch! Two enormous skate on display on the west beach, c.1995.

myself ready to start from Lynmouth Quay in weather of the most beautiful description. A sea like oil, and the first gleams of the sun rising over Countisbury Hill, even without the fishing, made the morning one to be enjoyed and remembered.

We set off in the trim *Kingfisher* with Mr Bevan at the rudder and two sturdy, though quite young, experienced boatmen, who beat cheerfully to their oars... The fog of the previous night, when the 'spiller' was set, had made its whereabouts a little uncertain, and half an hour was spent in rowing about before the buoy marking the end of the line was found. I must explain that the 'spiller' consists of a strong line, almost the thickness of a leadline, 400 yards long, and carries at each fathom a short length of cod-line with a strong brass swivel, and an inch Limerick hook baited with a piece of fresh herring, and anchored at each end across the tide by a heavy grapnel with a cork buoy attached to each end of the line. As soon as the tide eases off the cork buoy bobs up, and the moment for drawing the 'spiller' arrives...

In a few seconds a splashing announces that something is coming up, and the gaff is called into requisition to land a skate about 2ft 6in across the 'wings'. He is dropped into a sort of well between the thwarts, and more line hauled in. Now a dogfish, now another, now a conger about 3ft long (not big enough to give trouble), then a small skate, then congers one, two, three, and so on, till a mighty splash makes us look over the side

A 'monster from the deep'.

to see a regular 50-pounder into whose side the gaff is stuck, and who takes the united efforts of the captain and half the crew to bring on board. A hitch is given round a thole pin, and many whacks bestowed on the conger. Still he bangs and slides about till he goes overboard, but is quickly regaffed and brought back into the well, where he lies among his fellows in misfortune till a few more are piled on him, when he sets up a squirming that upheaves the whole mass, which gurgles and barks and twists until brought to a sense of duty by unlimited applications of the butt end of the gaffe.

Now comes up a deep-sea blue shark, only 2ft long, but the real article which we know out in the ocean; then a small conger or two, a dogfish 4ft long, several large skate, and then the crowning monster skate of 106lb weight. Something like a fish, and what is more, very good to eat, as we found later, and worthy of the photography which he undergoes. With a few small additions, the rest of the line is hauled on board, and thoughts of breakfast fill our breasts, and so homeward bound we pull smartly along. As soon as we reach shore the steelyard is called into play, and over 5cwt of good eatable fish is found to be the result of our expedition. On other expeditions some skate have been caught by Mr Bevan of 196lb weight.

Of course, the sporting element is not so great as in hand-line fishing, but still the excitement of the speculation as to the catch is well worth the effort of going out, even if we had not the genial good fellowship of the skipper of the *Kingfisher* to add to the pleasure of the trip... I can recommend anyone visiting this part of the world to make friends with Mr Bevan and to ask permission to take part in his daily forays against the monsters of the deep.

Unidentified Newspaper Cutting, Autumn 1901

Stagecoaches

Coach Travel in 1853

DR THOMAS COOPER'S guidebook provides some interesting information about travel in the early 1850s. We learn that by this time there were public coach services to and from a number of towns, and that on most coaches inside seats cost more. Seats on top were usually not quite so expensive, passengers up there being exposed to the weather, though they did have the best views:

A four-horse coach leaving Lynton, 1859.

To Barnstaple, Richards' Omnibus starts from the Lynton Post Office, on Tuesday and Friday mornings at 6, reaching Barnstaple in time for the Tiverton and Plymouth coaches, returning from the King's Arms the

LYNTON AND MINEHEAD.
THE
FAVOURITE SEASON COACH,
"LORNA DOONE,"

Commenced running between ROYAL CASTLE HOTEL, Lynton, and Railway Station, Minehead, on the 26th April. For particulars see Great Western Railway Time Tables and bills.

T. BAKER, Jun., Proprietor.
Dated Private Hotel, Lynton, 14th April, 1886.

Lynton, Lynmouth, and Barnstaple.

THE QUICKEST ROUTE BY THREE-QUARTERS OF AN HOUR.

A FAST FOUR-HORSE COACH
(Carrying the Mails)

RUNS DAILY throughout the year, in connection with the through Fast Train of the London and South Western Railway, passing through some of the finest scenery in Devonshire.

	UP.		
Depart from Lynton	...	...	8 0 a.m.
Arrive Barnstaple ...	...	...	10 55 a.m.
Depart "	...	...	11 3 a.m.
Arrive Waterloo	...	...	5 17 p.m.

	DOWN.		
Depart from Waterloo ...	...	...	9 0 a.m.
Arrive Barnstaple ...	...	...	3 21 p.m.
Depart "	...	...	3 40 p.m.
Arrive Lynton...	..	...	6 30 p.m.

Booking Office:—L. & S.W.R., Church Hill, Lynton.

JONES BROS.,
PROPRIETORS.

Advertisements for two of Lynton's most important coach services, Ilfracombe Chronicle, *24 July 1886.*

A coach leaving Ilfracombe for Lynton in the Edwardian era.

Coach descending Lynmouth Hill, 1911. Drags were fixed to the back wheels. The unmade road became deeply rutted.

An Ilfracombe to Lynton coach at Parracombe in the Edwardian era.

same afternoon at three o'clock. The fare is two shillings and sixpence. To Ilfracombe an omnibus runs three times a week, Monday, Wednesday and Friday, starting at 11 o'clock from the Crown Hotel, Lynton, and returning the following day from the Clarence Hotel, during the months of June, July, August and September; the fare is 4 shillings outside and 5 shillings inside.

During the Summer months also, from the beginning of June to the middle of October, a coach runs daily (starting at 6 o'clock in the morning and returning at half-past 8) through Porlock, Minehead and Dunster, to Bridgwater; another meets this coach at Minehead for Taunton, both arriving at their respective destinations in time to meet the Express Train from Exeter to London. They again start upon their homeward journey upon the arrival of the Express Train down, from London. The fare is 12 shillings outside and 20 shillings inside.

T.H.Cooper, A Guide Containing a Short Historical Sketch of Lynton and Lynmouth (1853)

The Minehead coach about to leave the Royal Castle Hotel.

A Restrained Coach Driver!

Many amusing tales were told of the early coach drivers. Perhaps the best was that related by the Revd Thornton, curate of Countisbury, about his coach journey in the mid-1850s when he went to meet the train at Bridgwater Station:

> Those drivers of old North Devon were wonderful men. There was one Warwell, who drove the coach from Lynton to Bridgwater. I once started with him very early in the morning to meet my two nieces from London. We left Lynton about six a.m., and Warwell had beer at Countesbury, beer again at Porlock, Minehead, Dunster, Williton, Putsham and Cannington. What he consumed in the couple of hours during which the coach waited at Bridgwater I do not know, but on the return journey he had hot

The Minehead coach at Lynmouth. The extra pair of horses were needed for the climb up Countisbury Hill.

spirits at every place where in the forenoon he had called for beer. We reached Lynton at about ten p.m., and he congratulated himself to me on his self-restraint in the matter of drink. He never took spirits until he turned backwards, as some people did; but he could never abide their drinking ways, so he said.

W.H.Thornton, Reminiscences and Reflections of an Old West-Country Clergyman (1897), Vol. 1

An Exceptional Coach Service

By the late-nineteenth century Lynton and Lynmouth had one of the finest coach services in the country. Seaside resorts in more densely populated districts had lost most of their coaches when they obtained rail links, but from Lynton and Lynmouth horse-drawn coaches still ran over the hills to connect with trains at the railway stations. The coaches swayed from side to side and bumped over every stone and rut in the road, but many tourists saw them as an important attraction. In July 1890 the *Lynton and Lynmouth Recorder* boasted about the remarkable number of coaches serving the resort:

The Minehead coach outside the Lyndale Hotel, Lynmouth in 1892.

A coach makes its way up Countisbury Hill.

Countisbury, 1907. The coach at the Blue Ball Inn (now the Exmoor Sandpiper).

If Lynton is blest with anything it is its grand scenery and its splendid coach service which is as complete as it well can be with one exception. Such a service of coaches we know not another place in England possessing.

To Barnstaple we have Jones Bros' three coaches, viz: *Tantivy* at 8 a.m.; *Glen Lyn* at 12 p.m.; *Tally Ho!* at 5 p.m.

To Minehead Mr T.Baker is running *Lorna Doone* from the Royal Castle Hotel at 9.30 a.m., and the *Red Deer* at 4 p.m. daily. The Valley Company are also running the coach *Valley of Rocks*.

From Lynmouth Mr W.Bevan is running over Exmoor to Dulverton a four-horse coach *Tally Ho!* Mondays, Wednesdays and Fridays, at 9.45 a.m.

Whilst to Ilfracombe we have six coaches daily: Mr J.Holman's fast four-horse coach *Forester* daily, leaving the Kensington Hotel at 5 p.m.;

Minehead Station in the Edwardian era. The coach from Lynton connected with a train here.

Lake and Copp's three coaches daily (Sundays excepted) — the *Dreadnought* leaves the Valley of Rocks Hotel at 9.30 a.m.; the *Defiance* at 5 p.m.; the *Katerfelto* leaves the Bath Hotel, Lynmouth at 5 p.m.; the *Teazer*, Lovering and Son, Proprietors, leaves the Kensington Hotel at 5 p.m. Last but not least is our old friend Sam Colwill's *Benita*, which has been on the road for over 30 years, leaving the Royal Castle Hotel at 5 p.m. daily.

But the one exception before mentioned is the South Molton route, its scenery by the Bray Valley is so very pretty that we wonder much that no coach has been placed on that road, but now to complete the last link in the coach service, Mr T.Baker has started the *Wild West* from Dulverton.

Lynton and Lynmouth Recorder, 15 July 1890

More Rivalry

Many of the coaches finished their journey to Lynton and Lynmouth outside a particular hotel. This was not an accident. Local hoteliers often operated, backed

Coaches about to leave Jones's coach office, 1911.

Coach outside the Valley of Rocks Hotel in the early 20th century.

Advertisement for Tom Jones's horse-drawn coach trips, 1904.

or at least supported particular coach services in the hope that these coaches would bring them customers. Passengers sometimes grumbled that they were being pressurised into patronising certain hotels, just as people travelling in private carriages had complained of similar treatment many years earlier:

LYNTON.

8 Coaching Trips

FROM LYNTON,

LEAVING THE
ROYAL CASTLE HOTEL, DURING THE SUMMER MONTHS.

A **Char-a-banc** runs daily at **11** a.m., to **Doone Valley**, return fare **4/-**

A **Char-a-banc** runs Tuesdays, Thursdays and Saturdays **11** a.m., to **Hunter's Inn** *via* **Wooda Bay** for **Heddons Mouth**, return fare **4/-**

The **Four-Horse Coach "Lyn,"** runs Mondays and Thursdays at **9.45**, to **Ilfracombe** *via* **Combe Martin** and **Watermouth Castle**, return fare **6/-**

A **Char-a-banc** runs on Wednesday at **11** a.m., to **Porlock**, return fare **4/6**

A **Char-a-banc** runs on Fridays at **11** a.m., to **Simonsbath**, return fare **4/-**

The **Four-Horse Coach "Lorna Doone"** runs daily at **9.15** a.m., and **"Red Deer,"** **4.30** p.m., to **Minehead**, return fare **9/-**

A **Char-a-banc** runs daily at **1.30**, to **Valley Rock** and **Watersmeet**, return fare, **2/6.**

'BUS MEETS ALL PRINCIPAL TRAINS.

Private Carriages (opened or closed) to meet any train at Lynton, Barnstaple, Minehead, or Ilfracombe, on receipt of Wire. Telegrams—Tom Jones, Lynton. Agent for Lynton and Barnstaple Railway. Furniture Removed and Warehoused. Char-a-bancs run to the Meets of the Devon and Somerset Staghounds at Cloutsham, Yearnor Moor. Brendon Two Gates, Hawkcombe Head, &c.

DEVONSHIRE COBS FOR HUNTING OR HACKING.
HORSES FOR DRIVING BY DAY OR JOB.

BOOK SEATS AT . . .
JONES'S COACH OFFICE,
CHURCH HILL, LYNTON.

> By 20 miles of picturesque but trying road, crowded coaches arrive in the season from the four nearest stations — Ilfracombe, Minehead, Barnstaple and Dulverton. As to a choice among rival vehicles, the public should be warned that jealousy seems to run rather high between rival hotels, and some of the coaches being the enterprise of certain landlords, the passenger must make sure beforehand of not being carried beyond his intended halting-place, and having his luggage set down on the road in dust or rain, with the apparent view of driving him into another haven.

> A.R.H. Moncrieff, *Where Shall We Go?* (1892)

Paddle-Steamers

THOUSANDS OF visitors enjoyed their first view of the twin villages from out in Lynmouth Bay, for the difficulties of land access caused many to opt to travel there by sea. In the early days sea travel was an adventure, but a slow one, for sailing vessels were often delayed by adverse winds or tides.

Paddle-steamers first began operating on Bristol Channel routes in the 1820s. By 1830 the steamer *Glamorgan* was calling at Lynmouth on its journey between Bristol and Ilfracombe. In the following decade steamers on the Bristol to Bideford and Bristol to Hayle services also began to drop passengers at Lynmouth. These steamers operated to a proper summer timetable and provided a cheap and convenient way of travelling to the resort.

Landing Difficulties

Lynmouth was handicapped because it lacked a deep-water harbour. Steamers had to anchor in the bay while passengers were ferried ashore in small craft. Dr Cooper's guidebook gives details of the steamer services in 1853 and describes the problems passengers faced when the sea was rough:

> Steamers, running every week from Bristol to Cornwall, call off the shore, landing passengers in boats. They start from Bristol at high-water, arriving in six hours, which then is low-water at Lynmouth, so that boats are required for landing; but if the sea is very rough this is rendered impossible, owing to the heavy surf then off the shore; in such a case, the passengers are obliged to proceed on to Ilfracombe, and occasionally from the same cause they have been obliged to go on to Cornwall...
>
> During the Summer, a steamer runs twice a week from Bideford to Bristol and back, calling off Lynmouth, unless the weather is too rough to land the passengers. The fare is, chief cabin 8 shillings, and deck 5 shillings, together with the charge of landing. Mr George Fry, draper, Lynton, is agent.
>
> T.H.Cooper, A Guide Containing a Short Historical Sketch of Lynton and Lynmouth (1853)

A steamer advertisement, 1849. Passengers are warned that they will not be landed at Lynmouth if the sea is rough.

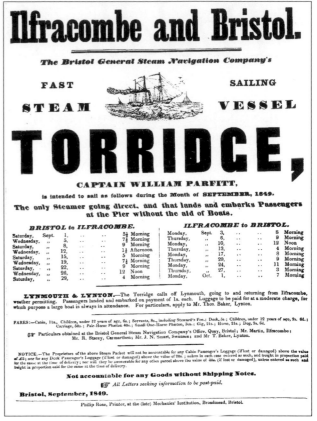

The Steamer from Portishead

In 1869 the journey from Bristol to Lynmouth was made much quicker by the opening of a pier at Portishead. Passengers could now travel to Portishead by train on the new railway from Bristol and catch the steamer at the pier, thus cutting out the long, slow steamer journey they had previously had to make down the Avon from Bristol.

Steamers setting off from Bristol had always had to leave Bristol at high water so they could negotiate the Avon. In 1870, however, Portishead pier was given a deep-water extension, which meant that steamers could call at any state of the tide and thus departures from there could be at the same time each day. By July 1870 the Cardiff and Portishead Steamship Company was advertising that its steamer *Ely* would leave Portishead at 1.30 p.m. each day, after the arrival of Midland Railway trains from Derby and Birmingham, and a Great Western Railway train from Paddington, and would call off Lynmouth on its way to Ilfracombe.

The following account was written by a tourist who travelled from Portishead to Lynmouth on the steamer *Ely* at the height of the summer season in 1877:

> What may be the specific gravity of the river Severn off Portishead, I've no idea. It is simply a drab liquid road, a whitey-brown bog — too unsafe to drive a coach over, but powerfully nasty stuff for a steamer to get through, even with wheels…
>
> But at Weston the water begins to feel the power of Atlantic dilution, and off Watchet it is almost clear. From that point the huge rusty hills of

North Devon come looming along on the coast, you can see green sea, can draw a long breath, feel fresh air, and indignantly eject from your lungs (stomach, if preferred, as too many of my fellow-pilgrims did) the last reminiscences of Bristol.

Lynmouth was my haven; and I was rather disappointed on looking at it from the sea in the gloom of the evening. But it's a place that will stand a deal of looking at, and the more you look at it the more there is to see. The worst of it is it is too popular, and therefore too much over-run. Tourists are as plentiful as wasps.

As to lodgings, after a weary search, along with the heavy contingent poured in by the steamer *Ely*, I came to the conclusion, on reliable information, that there was only one bed-room and one sitting room available for me in the place, which of course I secured — for the hotel had long given up indoor maintenance, and was at its wits' end to provide even outdoor relief for applicants.

It was Saturday night when I arrived; there was not a scrap of meat in the village, and the butcher had shut up shop. He was, however, ultimately coaxed to come out and kill another sheep expressly for me and my fellow immigrants.

North Devon Herald, 11 October 1877

The Excursion Steamer

From the 1840s onwards excursion steamers occasionally brought day-trippers to Lynton and Lynmouth. These cheap day-trips appealed mainly to the working classes, whereas the regular steamer services were patronised mainly by the wealthy long-stay visitors. A problem occasionally arose when the day-trippers were being ferried between the steamer and the shore. Whereas advertisements for the regular steamers made it clear there would be an additional fare payable for the landing service, this was not always the case with excursions.

The following report refers to an occasion when a dispute arose over a charge made to a group of day-trippers:

The *Prince of Wales* passenger boat left Bideford on Friday morning on an excursion to Lynton, calling at Ilfracombe on the way, when the company,

61

although not very large, was respectable, and the trip was a most pleasant and agreeable one. The weather being remarkably fine, the splendid scenery of Lynton was seen to advantage, and during the four hours' stay the principal places of interest were visited, the only drawback being the scandalous way in which people are imposed on by the inhabitants of the place, who take every advantage of strangers. The exorbitant charges made for everything and every accommodation was the subject of general complaint, and the hotel charges were positively outrageous.

On leaving Lynton the party were subject to another imposition, which was denounced by one and all as a perfect swindle. The small boats off the beach having been well filled with the passengers ready for conveyance to the *Prince of Wales*, which was anchored a short distance out, a demand of sixpence from each person was made by the men, who not only indulged in offensive and insulting language, but threatened that if the demand was not complied with the party should be turned out of the boats and prevented from joining the steamer, which was then waiting

Passengers being ferried out to a steamer, c.1906.

to start on her return journey. The money was eventually paid with a general protest, inasmuch as the steam-packet company had undertaken to convey the passengers to and fro for a certain sum...

The arrangements on the *Prince of Wales*, however, gave every satisfaction. There was scarcely a ripple on the sea during the trip, and with the exception of the charges referred to, everything passed off satisfactorily, and the company thoroughly enjoyed themselves. The drum and fife band of the Bideford Volunteers was in attendance, and a professional singer enlivened the journey by singing several excellent songs to guitar accompaniment.

Bideford Weekly Gazette, 15 June 1869

Excursion Steamers Multiply

The late-nineteenth century was the golden age of the excursion steamer. They became such familiar sights that locals could identify each long, graceful vessel while it was still some way out. The following newspaper report shows that

Lynmouth, c.1920. Steamers called quite frequently.

excursion steamers called quite frequently at Lynmouth during the summer season, but passengers were not always able to land:

> The excursion steamers have been running regularly during the past week, and have landed a large number of visitors at Lynmouth. On Saturday there were three excursions from Bristol by the *Lorna Doone*, *Ravenswood* and *Waverley*. The *Earl of Dunraven*, from Cardiff, also landed a number of holiday keepers. On Monday many who came by the *Lorna Doone* were disappointed of landing at Lynmouth owing to the rough state of the sea.
>
> North Devon Journal, 9 June 1892

A New Curate Arrives

IN 1853 William Thornton graduated at Trinity College, Cambridge. Coming from a wealthy family, he could have looked forward to a life of leisure. However, he soon received a letter from Mr Halliday, the landed proprietor of Glenthorne, which was to change his life. Mr Halliday, an old family friend, was lord of the manor of Countisbury and in his letter he told this untried twenty-three-year-old that the curacy of Countisbury was his, if he wanted it:

One day in September I had a letter from Mr Halliday to say that Mr Mundy, the vicar of Lynton, wanted a curate, and that I could have the curacy, but that there would be no pay with it. My father, however, kindly said that he would allow me £200 a year.

I was enamoured of the West Country, and, therefore, agreed with Mr Mundy to take entire charge of the little parish of Countesbury, and to assist him sometimes at Lynton, for the modest stipend of twenty pounds a year. In October I passed the Voluntary Theological Examination, bought a big bay mare named 'Cochin China' and said goodbye to Cambridge...

After my ordination on a Sunday in Exeter Cathedral, I went to stay with Sir Thomas Acland, at Killerton, until Thursday, when, in floods of rain, I went to Crediton by rail, and there took coach for Barnstaple, driving on from thence to Lynton in a private conveyance. Mr Mundy took me in until I could secure lodgings... He was very kind, and kept me until a few days later when I had, ambitious young man as I was, taken a whole house called Island Cottage, consisting of two furnished sitting and five bedrooms, a kitchen, back kitchen and flower garden...

The house belonged to Mr Bevan, and his wife had once been cook to old Lord Castlereagh, and was a famous performer in her art. She kept a maid, and I had the whole furnished house, attendance, coals and garden for forty pounds a year!

'Cochin China' came down, together with a favourite white terrier with one black ear, named 'Crib'. So I hired a stable and engaged a young shoemaker to groom the mare. She cost me another £40, so that I had £120 to keep me in food, drink, clothes and travelling. I never was so rich in my life, and I have never lived so well. Mrs Bevan delighted in me, for I allowed her to do whatever she liked. I breakfasted late and heavily, at about half-past nine, and then required nothing more until I returned to dinner at about eight.

Soon she became famous for my dinner parties. I left all arrangements to her, and old Lord Castlereagh, Foreign Secretary of England, in all his glory, was not dined better than the curate and his friends; only, it was too magnificent.

If the women do not want to marry the men, at least they like to spoil them, especially curates; and with Mrs Bevan at my back, with her excellent cuisine, youth and good health on my side, a crack blood mare beneath me, keen professional inclinations and instincts, tempered by a strong love for rod, and gun, and hound, fondness for bird, and beast and plant, with Glenthorne always open to me... with a liking for solitude, and an aptitude for men and possibly for women, I was petted and made too much of.

In those days, at three-and-twenty, I knew no fear, and scoffed at fatigue, bad weather and exposure. Nothing came amiss, and I would walk, ride, shoot, fish, and drive with anybody. I was great, moreover, on the cliffs, and was never tired of risking my life, often alone, hanging and climbing in mid air on the Foreland, seeking for eggs.

The boatmen were fond of me, and many a stormy trip I made with them to Ilfracombe and elsewhere.

The wild shooting over the Glenthorne property (all Countesbury) was at my disposal. My basket would hold fourteen pounds weight of trout, and I thought scorn of the day on which I could not fill it...

I was keen in my parish work also. But what did I know about it?

William Thornton, 1890.

Lynmouth in 1870. The house on the right is Island Cottage, where William Thornton had lived.

Countesbury was handed over to me absolutely, weekday and Sunday alike, with its school and two hundred and fifty inhabitants. As to Lynton, with its two thousand, I might do what I pleased, much or little; but Countesbury was my own domain, and I was twenty-three; i.e. absolutely ignorant.

W.H.Thornton, Reminiscences and Reflections of an Old West-Country Clergyman (1897), Vol. 1

Royal Visits

An Incognito Visit

THERE WAS nothing like a royal visit to put a seaside resort on the map! Unfortunately, royal visits to Lynton and Lynmouth were few and far between. In the autumn of 1856, however, Lynton was visited by no less a person than Albert Edward, Prince of Wales. The future Edward VII was not quite 15. He strongly resembled his mother, reported the *North Devon Journal*, being 'not remarkably tall, rather delicately made, and of prepossessing appearance'. The prince was accompanied by his tutor and an attendant. They arrived at Barnstaple by train on a Saturday evening, supposedly incognito, and travelled to Lynton in a light carriage.

Lynmouth in 1865.

68

North Walk, c.1845.

After spending two nights at the Castle Hotel they rode to Ilfracombe and spent a night there, before leaving for Barnstaple where they caught the afternoon train:

Last Saturday evening Albert, Prince of Wales, with his tutor and attendance, stepped on the platform at the Barnstaple Station of the North Devon Railway, paying a visit incognito to this part of his future dominions.

Two gentlemen, a detachment from the Royal party, arrived here by the midday train, and hired a fly at Pridham and Lake's to carry on two gentlemen and a youth to Lynton, who would arrive by the 5.30 train. If we are rightly informed, the fly was not engaged until it was ascertained that there was no coach by which they could go on that evening, as had there been, three places were to have been engaged by them for that humbler mode of travel.

The Royal youth and his companions in travel arrived in due time, and proceeded on by the fly to Lynton. There being no appearance whatever of state, no one, not even David the driver, suspected what an important fare he was taking to the land of rocks. The Prince, it is said, was very affable, chatted familiarly on the way, made various inquiries respecting the owners of Arlington and other properties on the road. The Royal party halted at the London Inn, in Parracombe, and partook of some refreshments to the no small gratification of 'mine host', and thus baited, they proceeded to the Castle Hotel, where his Royal Highness remained during his stay at Lynton.

LYNTON, NORTH DEVON.

Baker's Royal Castle Hotel,

VISITED in September, 1856, by H. R. H. THE PRINCE OF WALES, and in May, 1862, by H. R. H. PRINCE ARTHUR. This Hotel affords first-rate accommodation to parties visiting this romantic neighbourhood. It is surrounded by its own grounds, the view from which is among the most magnificent in the kingdom, embracing Lynmouth, the Bristol Channel, Welsh Mountains, and Valleys of the Rocks, East and West Lynn, &c.

Coaches daily, during the Season, from this Hotel, to Ilfracombe and Barnstaple, and West Somerset Railway.

THOMAS BAKER, Proprietor.

Advertisement in a guidebook, 1870. Thomas Baker had renamed his hotel the Royal Castle Hotel.

On Monday morning the Prince and the gentlemen with him walked about and surveyed the romantic scenery of that startling locality, and in the afternoon, Mr Gibbs, his tutor, and the Hon. C.Leslie, hired three rough ponies and proceeded to Ilfracombe.

North Devon Journal, 9 October 1856

The Russian Princess

Foreign royalty occasionally visited the twin villages. On one occasion in the mid-1850s the Revd Thornton was called to the bath-house by the harbour to settle a dispute and found himself in the presence of a Russian princess. He changed her name when telling the tale:

> I one day received a call from a man who is still, in 1897, a dear friend. Mrs Bevan's little maid brought up a card to me as I sat in my drawing room at Island Cottage, and told me that a gentleman was waiting below to see me. The card belonged to the Rev. J.M.Dixon, of Holy Trinity, Bath; and the maid soon brought a fine, handsome, stout clergyman, of middle age, into the room, who immediately requested me to assist a brother in distress.
>
> He had with him, he said, a Russian princess, and she, walking by the pier at Lynmouth, had seen a notice in the window of the post office announcing that the owner of the house, a Mrs Trix, supplied visitors with baths of hot and cold sea-water. The princess inquired what the price would be, and was told that it was half-a-crown, whereupon she ordered one to be prepared, and bathed. But, said Mr Dixon, she is now very angry, and with good reason, for Mrs Trix wants her to pay ten shillings. So he begged me to go to my parishioner and to remonstrate with her, to induce her to accept half-a-crown; and I, being at that time young and foolish, consented, and went down the road to the attack, with the fine form of Mr Dixon covering my rear.

Lynmouth, c.1853. Mr and Mrs Trix's establishment is on the far right. Sea-water baths could be had there.

Mrs Trix, stood, with her arms akimbo, just outside her shop and library. She was a very little woman of fifty years, but of a fierce and very determined appearance. I ranged up alongside and opened fire, when the following dialogue ensued:-

'Is not your charge for a warm bath half-a-crown, Mrs Trix?'

'Yes certainly; you can see that it is so by looking at the card in the window of the bath-room.'

'But, Mrs Trix, the Princess Poniatowski says that you have charged her ten shillings; and she is very angry, and declares that she will not pay. How is it that you charge her so much?'

'Well, sir, nothing is too good for these foreigners, and she made me put fresh curtains in the windows, fresh carpets on the floor, and provide her with relays of hot water, and a succession of hot towels. I shall be badly remunerated with ten shillings for my trouble, I am sure.'

Just then Mr Dixon interposed with an unfortunate remark, 'The princess also complains that the bath was dirty, Mrs Trix.'

'Dirty!' screamed the indignant little woman. 'If it was dirty when she went in, what do you imagine, sir, was its condition by the time she came out?'

This was too much for me, and I fled in wild confusion, routed, down the street, with the rear-guard clattering at my heels, leaving the female combatant in triumphant possession of the field; a lady, worthy, shall I say, of the order of the Bath? And the princess had to pay her demand.

> *Post Office, Lynmouth.*
> **TRIX,**
> TEA DEALER, GROCER, STATIONER, &c.,
> Pickles, Fish Sauces, Spices, Jellies, Jams, Marmalade ; Schweppe's Soda Water, and Lemonade ; Snuffs and Cigars ; Wax, Sperm, and Composition Candles ; Drawing Materials ; Perfumery ; Lynton and Lynmouth Views ; Guides, &c. ; a good assortment of Artificial Flies ; Salt Water Baths ; Circulating Library, with many other Articles too numerous to particularize.

Advertisement in Bright's Intelligencer for Ilfracombe and Lynton and Lynmouth, *27 July 1860. Mr and Mrs Trix offered a remarkable range of goods and services.*

W.H.Thornton, Reminiscences and Reflections of an Old West-Country Clergyman (1897), Vol. 1

The Future Kaiser Calls

In September 1878 another royal tourist made a fleeting visit to Lynton. His Imperial Highness Prince Frederick William of Prussia was nineteen at the time and was holidaying at Ilfracombe when he decided to make a day visit to Lynton:

> Lynton. — The season of 1878 has been a very prosperous one for this rising and deservedly admired watering place… Amongst the many distinguished visitors it has had this season was Prince Frederick William of Prussia, who paid a flying visit here on Monday week, and who was charmed with the scenery, through which he was piloted by Mr Crook, of the Valley of Rocks Hotel.
>
> North Devon Journal, 26 September 1878

Ten years later this young man was crowned Kaiser. In 1914 he became the most hated man in Britain, but by then few Lyntonians remembered that he had once been an honoured visitor to their town.

Floods

MOST PEOPLE have heard of the Lynmouth flood of 1952, but perhaps they are not aware that in earlier years the village suffered both river and sea floods.

The Great Storm of 1607

In 1607 a combination of fierce gale and an abnormally high tide caused havoc at Lynmouth:

> Much of the older part of Lynmouth, owing to the huts being imprudently built too near the sea, was in 1607 washed away in a gale at the time of a spring tide… Amongst the houses then destroyed was an entire row of cottages, which stood along the shore where now the sea wall is built, forming one side of the field whereon the house of Mr Roe stands.
>
> T.H.Cooper, A Guide Containing a Short Historical Sketch of Lynton and Lynmouth (1853)

Heavy seas at Lynmouth. Notice the debris on the esplanade.

Damage to the Harbour

In the early summer of 1770 Lynmouth was again hit, this time by a serious river flood which dumped boulders similar in size to those carried down in the flood disaster of 1952.

The seamen of Lynmouth petitioned the lord of the manor, who lived in Exeter, hoping he would take pity on them and help pay for essential repairs to the badly damaged harbour. Twenty-seven inhabitants signed the petition, twenty-two in their own handwriting, one putting his letters, and four making their mark:

To John Short Esq. — The Humble Petition of the Seamen of Limouth on behalf of themselves and other inhabitants of Linton and Limouth aforesaid humbly sheweth –

That the river at Limouth by the late rain rose to such a degree as was never known by the memory of any man now living, which brought down great rocks of several tons each, and choaked up the harbour; broke one boat to pieces and was driven to sea, and another boat was driven on the rocks which cost upwards of twelve pounds in repairing; and had all the rest been there, some of them must have been broken to pieces and driven away, and perhaps several people drowned (as some was then likely to be) which would have been the destruction of many families. And also carried away the foundation under the Kay on that side against the river six foot down and ninety foot long, and some places two foot in under the Kay, which stands now in great danger of falling. And had it not been for a new Kay adjoining to the head of the other, of seventy foot long and four foot high, made last winter with large rocks, and at the entire expense and labour of the seamen, the Kay head would have actually been down, as the river forced itself that way and the rest must soon have followed after.

And as the place is now so ruinous, the seamen and other families must entirely leave it, and then it will all soon be washed away if not immediately repaired, which by a moderate computation will amount to forty pounds. Therefore the said petitioners humbly desire your honour to advance what your goodness shall think proper, as they will advance and do what lieth in their power, which may be of advantage to you and your posterity, and your petitioners as in duty bound will ever pray.

Devon Record Office, 52/14/2/1, Humble Petition of the Seamen of Limouth, 8 August 1770

The River Flood of 1859

In late October 1859 the Lyn again flooded. By this time buildings had been erected along the river so, although the river never developed the destructive force of 1770, it still caused considerable damage:

Lynmouth, 1865. Buildings close to the river are at risk if the river floods.

On Tuesday evening, the 25th ult., the inhabitants of Lynmouth were greatly alarmed by the overflowing of the river Lynn, owing to the quantity of snow that was gathered on the moor, and the heavy rains on Tuesday. It rose so rapidly as to drive all before it. The yards and stables belonging to the Lyndale Hotel were filled with water to the height of three or four feet. All the back premises of Mr Wm. Richards were washed away, together with a quantity of beer and brewing utensils. The back houses of Mr H.Bale and Mr Thomas Bevan were also carried away. The loss is estimated at about £300.

In the evening, just as the gale was at its height, the smack *Mary*, William Groves, master, came into harbour, all safe, from Newport. The oldest man now living at Lynmouth never saw the river Lynn rise to such a height before. We are happy to say that no lives were lost although several had narrow escapes.

North Devon Journal, 3 November 1859

The Gale of 1910

In December 1910 a severe gale whipped up huge seas in the Bristol Channel. The two newspaper accounts which follow describe the damage at Lynmouth:

On Friday evening the high tide, big river, and westerly wind, combined to produce at Lynmouth a flood quite unprecedented in the memory of any living person. At six o'clock, when it was high water, the tide rushed up the harbour, absolutely filling it, and overflowing into the main street

Storm damage at Nelson Cottage, Lynmouth, December 1910, showing the wall that fell 'with a shot like the report of a gun'.

from the Rising Sun to Mr E.J.Pedder's coal stores. A boat could easily have floated up the street for the whole distance. The houses in the locality were all flooded, there being three feet of water in some...

A damaged boat washed up by the lime kilns after the storm of 1910.

The greatest destruction, however, was caused at Mr H.Moore's Nelson Cottage. Here the whole wall facing the Bath Hotel was swept

*Nelson Cottage, 1910.
Another picture of the
storm damage.*

down in a block
— falling with a
shot like the
report of a gun.
On the river
side the wall
went down also,
and the sea
poured all over

the lawn and garden, rooting up everything in its way, working
devastation.

Storm damage on the esplanade, 1910.

Huge masses of water swept over the wooden bridge and far upstream. Against the Esplanade they thundered, but the splendid wall withstood them nobly. The road inside, however, was scooped out in enormous holes and literally covered with tons of rock and debris.

North Devon Herald, 22 December 1910

The fence at the foot of the Cliff Railway was washed away, while the violence of the storm is evidenced by the fact that part of the stack of bricks and tiles, situate in the Cliff Railway yard, was washed half way up the village. The iron seats fixed to the foundation of the Esplanade-road were torn up and flung some distance, whilst boats lying on the Esplanade were flung up near the Cliff Railway, some being smashed to bits.

North Devon Journal, 22 December 1910

Lynmouth Coastal Traders

THROUGHOUT the nineteenth century Lynmouth was the home port for a few coastal trading vessels. The hilly country surrounding the twin villages meant it was easier to bring in bulky goods by sea rather than by the moorland roads. Sloops imported coal and limestone from Wales, food supplies and general goods from Bristol. From time to time these same vessels would take away pitprops and oak bark, the products of local oak woods.

There was always a temptation to overload the little cargo boats to increase the profit on each sailing. The crews knew that sudden storms could blow up on the Bristol Channel, but they accepted the risk of shipwreck as an inevitable hazard of their trade.

Lynmouth Harbour in the early 1880s.

Three cargo vessels in the harbour, c.1890.

A Vessel Sinks

The following account describes the sad loss of one Lynmouth trader in February 1869:

> The loss of the *Topsy*, of Lynmouth, which foundered off Minehead in the terrific gale of last Friday week, whereby four lives were lost, has cast a gloom over this place. For some days, great anxiety was felt as she was reported to have left Newport, and had not been heard of since; but it was not until Friday last that all hope was given up. She was seen rolling heavily in the sea under bare poles, when she suddenly sank without any hope of assistance. Her cargo consisted of coal, but beyond the fact of her being seen to founder, any further particulars as to her state and condition will never be ascertained, as all on board perished. Her crew consisted of the master, William Crocombe, and two seamen, George Groves and William Watty, and unfortunately they had a little boy called

Lynmouth in 1892. The pile of stones in the foreground might be there for use as ballast by departing vessels. New buildings are nearing completion on the esplanade.

Richards with them, to whom they were giving a passage home. Four families have been thrown into distress by this melancholy accident. William Crocombe leaves a young wife and two children. Groves a wife (very ill) and four children, in great poverty. A subscription has been started in aid of the widows and orphans, and much sympathy is felt and expressed towards them in their bereavement. Watty unfortunately was unmarried, but he leaves a father and mother to mourn his loss.

North Devon Journal, 25 February 1869

A Busy Harbour

Late in the nineteenth century the harbour was often the scene of bustling activity. The Cliff Railway was kept running in winter, as it provided the easiest way of transporting imported goods up the cliff to Lynton:

Lynmouth too with the lift running looks quite busy with five vessels in the harbour: *Nautilus* from Bristol with general cargo, *Mary* from Bristol

A vessel being unloaded in the early 1890s.

with general cargo, *Penguin* from Bridgwater with general cargo, *Little Jane* from Cardiff with coal, and the *Samuel* with a cargo of pitwood outward bound.

Lynton and Lynmouth Recorder, 24 February 1891

A Narrow Escape

In the following month one of the vessels named above narrowly escaped disaster when trying to reach Lynmouth in bad weather:

During the terrible snowstorm of Monday, the smack *Mary* was sailing from Bristol to Lynmouth, laden with a general cargo. Soon after she rounded the Foreland a terrific gust of wind caught her, and tore away her mainsail and smashed other of her rigging. Great difficulty was experienced in getting her into Lynmouth harbour, but, by the united efforts of some Lynmouth seamen, she was safely harboured. The vessel is the property of Mr E.J.Pedder, of Lynmouth.

North Devon Journal, 19 March 1891

One of the mills on the Lyn system, c.1830. Flour was produced locally but many foodstuffs had to be brought in by sea.

A Coal Shortage

Before the opening of the Lynton and Barnstaple Railway almost all of the resort's coal was brought across the Bristol Channel from Wales. There was pressure on coal merchants to maintain supplies, but in adverse weather the coal boats found it very difficult to make port:

During the past week there has been quite a coal famine at Lynton and Lynmouth. The coal cellars had been emptied, and owing to the rough winds and consequently heavy sea the vessels were unable to land. On Friday last the *Little Jane* of Lynmouth, owned by Mr J.Crocombe and the *Mary* belonging to Mr E.J.Pedder, were towed down by a steam tug-boat. Both vessels were laden with coal, which was soon discharged at 23s. per ton.

North Devon Journal, 25 January 1895

A Vessel is Stranded

After the opening of the Lynton and Barnstaple Railway some coal was brought to the resorts by rail, but most merchants still found it cheaper and more convenient to bring in the fuel by sea. Occasionally there were still problems when the sailing vessels were trying to reach harbour:

The Lynmouth ketch, the *Three Sisters* became stranded opposite the salmon weir at the mouth of the Lyn, Lynmouth, early on Monday morning. The ketch, loaded with a cargo of Lydney coal for the owner,

Lynmouth after dark. Cargo vessels sometimes entered the harbour at night, if the tide was favourable.

Mr E.J.Pedder, was entering Lynmouth Harbour at 3 o'clock when it became stranded on the Western Ridge — the Esplanade side of the channel steamboat path.

There was a heavy ground-swell at the time and the vessel was in danger of breaking up. The boats of the vessel were already filled, and the crew, under Captain Sanders of Appledore, sounded the foghorn for assistance. The owner, Mr Pedder, with the coastguards, at once rowed out to the stranded vessel. Recognising the hopelessness of any attempts to refloat the ketch until the cargo had been discharged, Mr Pedder set a party of men to work and make a cart road over the Ridge. In response to Mr Pedder's appeals, the farmers of the neighbourhood lent their carts for the purpose of transferring the cargo to shore. The owner himself conducted the operations which evoked much applause from the large crowd of residents and visitors congregated on the Esplanade.

Within a few hours a large portion of the cargo was transferred to land, and the owner had the satisfaction of refloating the vessel at the next tide at 3 o'clock in the afternoon. Mr Pedder personally navigated the

Lynmouth, early in the 20th century. Vessels had to wait for the tide to enter and leave harbour.

vessel safely to the Quay, his arrival being the signal for hearty cheers from the crowd... The bottom of the vessel is badly damaged and unfortunately the damage is not covered by insurance. The cargo, however, is insured. Mr Pedder lost the *Mary* off the sand ridge only a few months ago. The sincere sympathy of everyone is extended to Mr Pedder in this further loss.

North Devon Journal, 23 June 1910

Cargoes of coal and other bulky goods continued to arrive by sea well into the present century. Indeed it was only the nationalisation of both coal and rail, soon after World War Two, which ended the sea-borne coal trade, for the Government then began to divert coal from privately-owned sea transport to state-owned rail transport.

Sea Rescues

The Valiant Boatmen of Lynmouth

SEVERAL TIMES in the nineteenth century the inhabitants of Lynmouth witnessed vessels being driven across the bay at the mercy of a storm. This is the Revd Thornton's description of one such incident in June 1854. The *Superb*, a small two-masted vessel, had set off from Barnstaple to sail to Bristol. No sooner had she reached the Bristol Channel than she encountered a heavy sea which carried away her masts and left her drifting at the mercy of a westerly gale:

> I was sitting in my room one stormy morning, when a great cry was raised in the street, and I was told there was a wreck in the bay. I hurried out under shelter of the low wall of the pier, and my heart grew sick within me as I saw a small vessel come round the rocks from the westward. She was about half a mile from land, her two masts were broken short off, and four human beings were lashed to their stumps. The top hamper was clinging to her side and causing her to lean over to leeward. A strong sea was running, with the current up channel, and two miles in front loomed the gigantic mass of the North Foreland,

Lynton and Lynmouth from Summerhouse Hill, c.1840. Many vessels sailed up and down the Bristol Channel.

Lynmouth Harbour, c.1880. On the quay stands the lifeboat house, a tall building which has not been whitewashed.

stretching far across the head of the bay. White foam was flecking its steep and murderous sides well nigh to the summit, one thousand two hundred feet above. One thing was manifest. No one could doubt the doom of crew and of vessel when those two short miles should have been traversed. Lynmouth at this time possessed no lifeboat, but many stout, broad-bottomed boats were in the river, or hard by on the shore.

The coastguard lieutenant, Hodges by name, was in bed with low fever... Presently from out of his bed, looking pale, but dressed very smartly, came the lieutenant and called for a crew. Eight men volunteered and stepped into a boat, as, also, did Mr Hodges, with the tiller in his hand. The men shewed no signs of excitement, they were rather more grumpy than usual, for they meant to risk their lives, and to do so with as little civility as possible, after the fashion of true-born Englishmen. There was no kissing of wives, no hugging of children, no hand-shaking with friends...

I shall never, never forget how that boat looked when the first wave

Lynmouth Harbour, c.1880.

caught her as she left the partial shelter of the pier. She stood up like a horse, and I thought she was gone, and all nine with her, but she righted, and the men pulled strong. Often we could not see anything of her in the trough of the waves, and then she would rise and ride over some great rolling pillow, only again to disappear.

Presently we saw her pass the wreck and come to on the further side. Then she returned, bringing with her two men, one woman, a boy and a shaggy dog. They were all nearly dead, for they had been drifting for a long time, and the human beings had been lashed to the masts and continually water washed. Then Lieutenant Hodges took off his wet clothes and went to bed to finish his fever comfortably. Dear old fellow, he was living a year or two ago, and for my part I could wish him immortal.

W.H.Thornton, Reminiscences and Reflections of an Old West-Country Clergyman (1897), Vol. 1

Preparing to launch the lifeboat, early in the 20th century. The lifeboat men are wearing cork jackets.

An Epic Lifeboat Rescue

Most people will have read an account of the epic lifeboat rescue performed by the Lynmouth crew on 12 January 1899. Here is a contemporary report from the *North Devon Journal*. It tells the story in a matter-of-fact way, but still succeeds in portraying the real heroism of the Lynmouth lifeboat men:

> Thursday last will long be remembered as one of the roughest experienced at Lynton and Lynmouth for a considerable time. There was a considerable gale blowing all day, and as a result the sea running was one of the roughest known on the coast for years. At about 7.52 p.m., Mr J.Crocombe, coxswain of the Lynmouth lifeboat, received two telegrams, one from the chief officer of the coastguard at Minehead and another from Mr Pollard, of Porlock, informing him that a vessel was in distress

near the latter place. Another wire was also received from Watchet stating that owing to the weather it was impossible to launch their lifeboat. The crew of the Lynmouth lifeboat were immediately summoned and quickly assembled.

The gale was now at its very worst, and it was at once seen it would be impossible to get the boat out at Lynmouth in the face of such a sea as was then running. A desperate move was then decided on, and the crew decided to take the boat overland to Porlock, and launch her from there. The tremendous difficulties to be overcome can only be realised by those who are acquainted with the road, which embraces 14 miles of the steepest and wildest country in England…

About a dozen horses were harnessed to the lifeboat, which, together with the carriage, weighs 10 tons, and with the assistance of a hundred men the journey was commenced. The difficulties to be encountered may be realised when it is mentioned that at two or three points the hedges had to be torn down to make room for the boat to pass, whilst at one point it had to be taken off the carriage and hauled along on skids for a considerable distance. All night the crew and a number of helpers were hard at work, and at 6.30 a.m. they reached Porlock.

Without waiting a moment Coxswain Crocombe and his crew put off and succeeded in reaching the ship, which proved to be the *Forrest Hall*, a large three-masted vessel of Liverpool, with a crew of thirteen men and five apprentices. The ship was a large one, of 1,900 tons register, and had left Bristol on Wednesday under the command of Captain Scott, in ballast, for Liverpool. She was being towed down Channel by the tug *Jane Joliffe*, and when near Lundy encountered such rough weather that it was decided to put back. Before this could be done, however, the hawser broke, and the tug becoming disabled had to leave the *Forrest Hall* to her fate. The steering gear of the vessel had also become disabled, and she was driven about at the mercy of the wind and tide, which carried her to a point about two miles north of Redstone, where her distress signals were sighted. When the lifeboat reached her she was riding with two anchors, and the Captain asked the crew to stand by him and establish communication with the shore and wire to Cardiff for tugs.

The *Jane Joliffe*, which had been compelled to abandon the ship the previous day, now came in search of her, and took her in tow. The crew of the lifeboat rendered considerable assistance in getting up the anchors and in seconding the efforts of the tug, the gale having again sprung up, and making the operation a most trying and most dangerous one. Owing to the force of the gale, and the damage to her steering equipment, it was impossible to put the bows of the ship round and she had to be towed almost the whole of the distance broadside on.

When within about a mile of the Nash Point, a second tug came to her assistance, and after seeing her safely brought up in Barry Roads at 5 o'clock, the lifeboat crew landed at Barry. The men were in an utterly exhausted condition, none of them having tasted food for twenty-four hours, and having undergone one of the most trying experiences it is possible to imagine...

The lifeboat returned to Lynmouth on Saturday morning, being towed down by a London steamer, the *Lasenbury*, bound for Genoa. The men, who all presented a weather-beaten appearance, were heartily glad to get safely home again.

North Devon Journal, 19 January 1899

Elevating The Masses: The Cliff Railway

EARLY IN September 1887 George Newnes made his first visit to Lynton and Lynmouth. This dynamic businessman had recently made a fortune based on the success of *Tit-Bits*, the working man's journal he had founded only six years earlier. He arrived seeking rest and relaxation, but instead found himself involved in an exciting new project.

Donkeys waiting patiently for work. It appears that the first part of the esplanade is being constructed, suggesting that the date is 1887.

The Lynton Station as the Cliff Railway nears completion, early in 1890.

Newnes came at the invitation of Thomas Hewitt, a successful lawyer who spent his summers at the Hoe on North Walk. In the previous year Hewitt had obtained an Act of Parliament enabling him to build an esplanade and pier at Lynmouth and a lift from Lynmouth to Lynton. The Lynton Local Board had already been persuaded to build the first part of the esplanade, and it is possible that Hewitt invited his wealthy friend to visit Lynton in the hope that he could be persuaded to put money into the rest of the project.

A trial run, early in 1890. Contractor's debris lies scattered around.

A trial run a few days before the official opening.

An Original Idea

The two men talked late into the night. It was the scheme for a cliff railway operated on the water-balance principle which appealed to George Newnes. Here was an original idea offering the chance of a good financial return. Once convinced he wasted no time. He acquired from Thomas Hewitt's company its legal powers to build a lift. Then he arranged that Bob Jones, partner in Jones Bros., local building contractors, would supervise the construction work. By December work was well under way:

> The excavation for the purpose of a hydraulic lift between Lynton and Lynmouth is steadily progressing. Many thousands of tons of material have been removed from the hillside.
>
> North Devon Journal, 8 December 1887

The First Cargo

The lift was being built mainly to transport passengers, but it was also intended that it should carry up to Lynton the bulky cargoes then arriving by sea at Lynmouth. In February 1890 the Cliff Railway at last neared completion and a cargo of cement provided the first freight to be taken up the cliff:

> The Cliff Railway is an accomplished fact. Cars have been run over the line during the past week, and the working of the railway has given general satisfaction. Jones Brothers received a cargo of cement at their Lynton stores by railway, this being the first actual employment in 'mineral' traffic. The transit of the whole cargo occupied five hours only, and a considerable economy of time and expense was consequently effected.
>
> North Devon Journal, 27 February 1890

The Opening Ceremony

The following extract comes from a newspaper report describing the official opening of the Cliff Railway on Easter Monday 1890 by Mrs Jeune, Lady of the Manor of Lynton:

The Cliff Railway soon after it opened. Building materials were brought by horse and cart from the harbour and were then taken on the lift to Lynton.

As the hour of the opening approached a large crowd gathered in the immediate vicinity of the Lynton Station of the Railway, all the coigns of vantage being early acquired, while the rustic bridges over the track were peopled with sightseers. There was also a numerous gathering at the Lynmouth Station. On the picturesque procession (headed by the Lynton Brass Band playing a stirring marching tune) appearing in sight, the car which was to perform the first journey received its full complement of passengers, ladies and gentlemen connected with the Press occupying the greater number of seats...

Mr Newnes then conducted Mrs Jeune to the raised dais under the wall of the reservoir from which the cistern of the car is filled. The little daughter of Mr Bob Jones, prettily attired, now stepped forward and presented Mrs Jeune with a beautiful bouquet of flowers. Graciously receiving the floral gift, that lady said: 'I have much pleasure in declaring the Cliff Railway open for public use, and I wish it every success.'

Pulling a lever placed over the dais, Mrs Jeune released the first car, which glided forward on its downward journey, a second car simultaneously starting on the upward track from Lynmouth. A Royal salute was fired by the Coastguardsmen, the bands played the National Anthem, and ringing cheers greeted the successful opening. When the cars met there was a similar demonstration, and on each arriving at its journey's end the crowds awoke the echoes again. The passengers, alighting, were loud in praise of the ease and pleasure of the motion and the magnificence of the view 'up along' and 'down along'. In this very gratifying way the opening of the Lynton and Lynmouth Cliff Railway was accomplished on Easter Monday.

North Devon Journal, 10 April 1890

Following the opening ceremony a luncheon as held at the Valley of Rocks Hotel. There George Newnes delighted most of his audience when he promised to give 'every possible assistance' to a project for the provision of a deep-water pier at Lynmouth. The tradespeople were ecstatic. For so many years they had longed for good landing facilities to encourage more steamers to call. Now it seemed their dreams would become reality.

Progress?

IN THE YEARS between 1886 and 1891 new buildings were erected at a rate never previously experienced in Lynton and Lynmouth. Encouraged by proposals for both a pier and a railway, and by the construction of a cliff railway, many local businessmen began to build new hotels, shops and houses in the confident expectation that tourists would flood in and good times lay ahead.

Most of the local tradesmen hailed this development as 'progress'. Yet some visitors were saddened to see quaint cottages being knocked down to make way for

Lynmouth, c.1880. The manor house is on the left. Above it stands the Tors, a wooded hillside which has yet to be built on.

modern structures, and new buildings being erected in areas of scenic beauty. The extracts which follow are chosen to reflect these different views.

Lynmouth in the mid 1890s. By this time the Tors Hotel and a few large villas have been built on the Tors.

Development on the Tors

In December 1886 William Bevan, a Lynmouth builder who owned the Lyndale Hotel, placed an advertisement in the local press. It related to the Tors estate overlooking Lynmouth. After leasing this undeveloped hillside from the lady of the manor in 1885, William Bevan had built the Tors Hotel in a prominent position. Now he was trying to lease out other sites overlooking the bay for development:

Lynmouth, North Devon.

THE LYNDALE HOTEL
AND
TORS PARK PRIVATE HOTEL,
Under the same Management.

BEAUTIFULLY situated on an eminence facing the Bristol Channel, and commanding the finest uninterrupted views of the Sea, Mountains, Woods, and Landscape Scenery in the North of Devon, two minutes' walk from the beach, and overlooking the River Lyn.

COFFEE, SMOKING, READING AND LADIES' DRAWING ROOMS.

BATH ROOM.

GOOD SALMON and TROUT FISHING, Free for gentlemen staying at either of the Hotels.

LAWN TENNIS.

Cheap Boarding Terms.   Write for Tariff and Photo showing position of Hotels

Good Accommodation for Parties Visiting Lynmouth for the day.

71—70   WILLIAM BEVAN, Proprietor.

Advertisement in the Ilfracombe Chronicle, *4 October 1887. Both hotels were owned by William Bevan. The Tors Park Hotel (Tors Hotel) had opened in the previous year.*

> To be let on lease for a term of 99 years about 50 splendid building sites in Tors Park, all commanding uninterrupted sea and land views. A first-class investment never again to be met at such a flourishing seaside watering place as Lynmouth, where houses are generally in great demand now it is decided to bring the railway into Lynton and a new pier at Lynmouth. A private hotel and gentleman's residence has already been built on the property. Particulars from W.Bevan, Lyndale Hotel, Lynmouth.
>
> Lynton and Lynmouth Recorder, 14 December 1886

A Warning

Visitors who loved Lynmouth's scenery were dismayed when they learnt that there were plans to build there. A travel writer warned of the dangers:

> Surely Lynmouth never appeared more lovely than on the day we left it… Long, long may it retain its simple rustic old-world look and peace-giving quietude. Never may the screech of the steam whistle disturb the reposeful tranquillity of this secluded haven of rest and repose. Never may its romantic glens be scarred by the sacrilegious hands of the railway contractor — that sworn enemy of beauty, that apostle of utility and creator of ugliness…

The Tors Hotel, in the Edwardian era.

But yet more to be dreaded is the speculative builder, with his levelling mania, flattening, smoothing, and parading all around, raising stucco terraces and marine crescents, hideous to look upon, turning each seaside resort into one monotonous uniformity of common-place. Enterprising builders and civil engineers, without the assistance of the railway contractor, have a wonderful capacity for sweeping away ruthlessly all that is charming and natural, and converting a simple primitive fishing hamlet into a dreariness of staring houses, with fashionable hotels, esplanades, desirable villas, and the inevitable pier, with all the many other things that go to make a modern watering place; the result being that of course all individuality and character is for ever lost, every resort under the altered circumstance being as much like the other as these enterprising individuals can make it.

James J. Hissey, On the Box Seat (1886)

The Valley of Rocks Hotel, c.1865. Between 1887 and 1890 the old buildings would be demolished to make room for a grander hotel.

'Improvements'

While some complained bitterly about the threat to the wild beauty of the Tors, the *Lynton and Lynmouth Recorder* in January 1888 congratulated William Bevan on his enterprise, enthused over proposals for a pier, rejoiced that work had begun to construct a cliff railway, and considered other development projects to be 'improvements':

> In reviewing the events of the past year it must be gratifying to Lyntonians to see that a spirit of enterprise has at last been awakened in our midst. In the early spring of last year we noticed that Mr William Bevan of the Lyndale and Tors Park Hotels, was sparing no pains or expense in making the Tors Park, which was formerly a barren waste, into what might be described as a paradise of loveliness...
>
> Mr J.Crook, of the Valley of Rocks Hotel, has also made a handsome addition to his hotel, which was brought into use in July last. Mr

J.W. Holman has opened a fine new hotel, known as the 'Kensington'. All this speaks well for private enterprise...

Then again there is the grand Esplanade at Lynmouth, which was opened by Mr Pitt-Lewis, and which is, we believe, the first instalment of a grand Pier which is to be constructed running westwards of the present harbour. This is to be carried out by a company, as is also the Lift or Tramway to be constructed between Lynton and Lynmouth...

We think that while other towns in North Devon can boast of the improvements they have made during the past year, yet none of them can compare with Lynton.

Lynton and Lynmouth Recorder, 10 January 1888

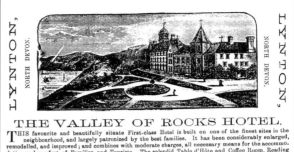

Advertisement for the Valley of Rocks Hotel in the Ilfracombe Chronicle, *4 October 1887. The far end of the building had been rebuilt earlier in the year.*

An advertisement in the Ilfracombe Chronicle, *28 August 1886, announces that the Kensington Boarding House (later known as the Imperial Hotel) will open in the following summer.*

Fatal Work

Louis Jennings, another travel writer, did not share this enthusiasm for development. When he visited Lynton and Lynmouth later in 1888 he was appalled at the damage being done to the natural landscape:

The hand of man is doing its usual fatal work on one of the loveliest spots our country had to boast of. Flaring notices everywhere proclaim the fact that building sites are procurable through the usual channels, this estate and the other has been laid out, the lady reduced in circumstances, and with spare rooms on her hands, watches you from behind the window-blinds, red cards are stuck in windows denoting that anything and everything is to be sold or let. A long and grievous gash has been torn in the side of the beautiful hill opposite Lynmouth — a gash which must leave behind it a broad deep scar never to be healed.

Louis J.Jennings, 'In The Wilds of North Devon', Murray's Magazine, IV (1888)

The Building Boom

Despite the protests, the building boom gathered pace and many businessmen rejoiced. In January 1890 a report in the *North Devon Journal* took pleasure in the fact that Lynton was beginning to expand westwards into what had been green fields, with houses being erected on a new road (Cross Street). It was also pleased to see buildings being put up in many other parts of the resort:

1889 has passed, leaving behind in Lynton signs of progress and improvement... Lyntonians are indebted to Mr Pedder for opening up a

Lynton from Hollerday Hill, 1871. In 1889 the village would begin to expand westwards into the meadows.

Lynbridge, c.1880. Some new houses would be erected here in the building boom of 1890-1891.

The Kensington Boarding House had fine sea views. In 1889 the owner of the adjacent Royal Castle Hotel erected a covered walkway right in front of the Kensington and this can be seen in the picture.

new road across Bate's meadow, conveniently connecting the Lee lane with Lydiate lane. The meadow is fast being built on. Only a small portion of the field is left for future disposal. Several tenements have been erected by the Valley of Rocks Hotel Company at Lynbridge; a fair sized villa residence on a nook at Westerway by Mr James Crocombe; also business houses and cottages by Messrs Heywood and Medway at Lynmouth. On the Tors Park estate building sites have been leased by Mr Bevan to the Rev. A.R.Hockley, and Messrs J.Crocombe, J.Hartnett, Legg and others. Already a colony of villa and cottage residences are dotting the hillside.

Most of the hotels have kept pace with the times and have improved their properties. The Valley of Rocks Hotel is constructing an entirely new wing. Many of the spacious rooms were ready for use during the season; the work will be completed in the early spring. The Royal Castle has opened a covered approach way from the hotel to the handsome billiard and smoking rooms; in front of the Kensington a promenade has been placed, commanding excellent sea views. The Crown Hotel has been provided with commercial and billiard rooms, also new stabling, laundry and bakery rooms. The Lyndale front has been improved, and a new bar and a well-fitted bagatelle room has been provided.

A great work and one likely to conduce to the future prosperity of Lynton is being carried out in the construction of a Cliff Railway. Arrangements are being made for the lighting of Lynton and Lynmouth by means of electricity.

North Devon Journal, 2 January 1890

The pace of development accelerated after the Cliff Railway opened at Easter 1890. It was given a further stimulus in 1891 when George Newnes obtained an Act empowering him to build a pier at Lynmouth. Businessmen staked their life-savings in new properties, confident that improved landing facilities would lead to large numbers of excursionists being landed by the steamers. By 1892 both Lynton and Lynmouth were spreading well beyond their former boundaries.

The Globe Hotel, c.1905. This hotel and the adjacent shops had been erected in the building boom of 1890-1891.

The 'Too Rapid March of Progress'

A.R.H.Moncrieff, another travel writer, was not impressed. He added his voice to those warning of the dangers of development:

> Some visitors, who would be more at home in Margate, complain bitterly that there is nothing to do of an evening. Other more congenial souls are rather inclined to cry out against the too rapid march of progress threatening to ruin the simple innocence of these retreats. Unsophisticated as they yet are, Lynmouth and Lynton boast the pride of electric lighting, and have lately been joined together, like Glion and Montreux, by a cliff railway or 'lift', a welcome aid to the rheumatic and short-winded, but a sore offence to some who, in every ominous placard offering eligible building sites, foresee the day when their beloved solitude

Lee Road, Lynton, c.1905. The town has extended westwards. In 1910 a Wesleyan Church would be built in the field on the right.

will be overwhelmed by bricks and stone and more and more invaded by exacting strangers.

A.R.H.Moncrieff, *Where Shall We Go?* (1892)

In February 1892 the bubble burst: George Newnes announced he was abandoning his plans to build a pier; property prices collapsed; speculators faced ruin; the building boom came to an abrupt end. Yet the clock could not

Lynmouth, 1919. The village has spread along the valley of the East Lyn.

be put back. Changes had been made and could not be reversed. The quaint old villages, so loved by artists, had been altered almost out of recognition. For better or worse, Lynton and Lynmouth had been transformed into a modern holiday resort.

Sam Colwill: Coachman

SAM COLWILL was the most celebrated whip ever to drive horse-drawn coaches to Lynton. Born in 1827, he had grown up in Ilfracombe. After a brief apprenticeship to a blacksmith, he had become a post boy, riding postilion for a coach and four. Then he had become a coachman, driving the Barnstaple to Bideford mail coach for Pridham and Lake, a leading North Devon coaching firm.

In 1854 Pridham and Lake gave Sam Colwill the honour of driving the first four-

Sam Colwill and his coach outside his booking office in Ilfracombe, c.1885. Every morning, except on Sundays, his coach set off for Lynton.

Changing horses at Easterclose Cross, above Combe Martin, on the road from Ilfracombe to Lynton.

horse coach between Ilfracombe and Lynton. This became his regular summer run, while in winter he drove the mail coach from Ilfracombe to Barnstaple. Then in 1874 the railway between Barnstaple and Ilfracombe was opened. Many people rejoiced, but not Sam Colwill, for he lost his regular winter employment, there no longer being a need for Pridham and Lake's coach service between the two towns.

The spread of the rail network meant hard times for most coachmen, but Sam Colwill was not a man to be beaten. Late in 1875 he took a big financial gamble, investing his life savings in the purchase of a small Ilfracombe coach company. Early in the following season he began running his own trips to Lynton, one of the few places still remote from the railway. His speculation paid off. In the years that followed Colwill's four-in-hand coaches would carry many thousands of visitors to the resort.

Early each morning the sound of the post horn announced the departure of the Lynton coach from Colwill's Booking Office in Ilfracombe High Street. There sat Sam on the box seat, proudly looking down on his team of magnificent greys. A gentle word, a shake of the reins and off rolled the coach on the first stage of its

An advertisement for Sam Colwill's coach in the Ilfracombe Chronicle, *24 July 1886.*

ENGLISH SWITZERLAND.

COLWILL'S
LYNTON AND LYNMOUTH

EXCURSION COACH "BENITA,"
OR A BREAK,
Will RUN EVERY DAY (Sundays excepted),
Driven by the Proprietor himself.
FARES 7s., including Coachman's Fees.

LEAVING the Ilfracombe Hotel at 8-30, and Colwill's ONLY Booking Office, directly opposite the Post Office, at 8-49 a.m.; Returning from Lynton at 6 p.m.

☞ *Book Early and ask for Colwill's Guide.*

For Single Fares, and arrangements for Families over Three in number, apply at
COLWILL'S ONLY BOOKING OFFICE,
96, HIGH STREET,
DIRECTLY OPPOSITE THE POST OFFICE.
POST HORSES and CARRIAGES, also a PONY CARRIAGE, LET ON HIRE.

S. COLWILL, Proprietor, 96, High Street, Ilfracombe; for more than 20 years Driver of the Barnstaple, Ilfracombe, and Lynton Coaches.

Passengers are requested to Note:—
☞ OPPOSITE THE POST OFFICE.

journey. At Easterclose Cross, above Combe Martin, there was a brief stop to enable the horses to be changed for a set of bays. After passing through Parracombe, the coach would eventually reach Lynton, the echo of the post horn on the surrounding hills announcing its arrival at the Royal Castle Hotel. A familiar figure in his tall top hat, Sam would then spend much of the afternoon swapping tales with cronies and exchanging a few words with visitors before returning to Ilfracombe in the early evening.

A ride on the box seat with Sam Colwell was a rare treat, for he was an encyclopedia of local lore, and enlivened the journey with a constant flow of information, reminiscences and anecdotes. His good humour and great skill as a whip made him a great favourite. Small wonder then, that rides on his coach, named the *Benita* after one of the characters in the *Lorna Doone* story, were always in demand. Another Ilfracombe firm, Lake and Copp, ran a rival coach, named the *Defiance*, on the same road, but Sam Colwill's fame usually ensured him the lion's share of the trade.

Sadly, at the age of 65, Sam's illustrious career as a coach driver came to a calamitous end. On the morning of Friday, 11 August 1893 he set off as usual from Ilfracombe to Lynton with a coach packed with holiday-makers, most of them ladies from London and Manchester. The top of Directions Hill, on the road from Lynbridge to Lynton, was reached without incident. There Sam was accustomed

Sam Colwill, a famous whip.

to apply the skids, which would dig into the unmade road and act as a brake. Not on that fateful morning:

A painful sensation was caused on Friday by an alarming coach accident which occurred at Lynton... The ample coach service between Ilfracombe and Lynton has long been immensely popular, and on Friday all the available accommodation was utilised. Mr Samuel Colwill has had such a long experience of coaching, and has secured such a wide reputation as a first-class whip, that there is generally keen competition for seats on the coach which he owns and drives, and on Friday the *Benita* had a full complement of eighteen passengers, many persons being disappointed because they had failed to secure seats in Colwill's coach.

Everything went smoothly until the end of the outward journey was almost reached and then an accident fraught with frightful possibilities happened... When nearing the top of Directions Hill — the steep declivity bounded on one side by the Glen Lyn ravine and on the other by the rock through which the road is cut, which has to be descended before the steep ascent to Lynton town is commenced — Colwill was about to stop as usual in order to have the drag adjusted, but before he could pull up, the horses were frightened by the waving of a little flag by a child in the roadway and by the shouting of other children. Alfred Sollis, the guard, at great personal risk, then attempted to fix the 'slipper' while the horses were in motion; he was unable to do this, and he at once

The front cover of a song about Sam Colwill, published after he died in 1919.

rushed to the horses' heads in the hope of being able to restrain them.

By this time, however, the coach was on the declivity, and there was no hope of stopping it. The horror and the difficulty of the situation were increased by the fact that just in front was Copp's *Defiance*, another fully laden coach.

In this awful crisis Colwill retained his coolness. He shouted to the driver of the coach in front to make way, and seeing that a smash was inevitable, strained every effort to keep the coach from crashing into the ravine, which is protected simply by a low wall of loose stones. The front right wheel of the *Benita* came into violent contact with the kerbing of the path, recently constructed by the side of the boundary wall, and this caused the coach to turn over, some of the passengers being precipitated into the roadway. The driver, Miss Jane Waugh, and Miss Elizabeth Watson, were precipitated over the wall into Glen Lyn, falling a distance of fifty feet. Three of the four horses dashed through the boundary wall, in which a breach of several yards was made, falling to the first ledge and crashing through the brushwood to the stream at the bottom of the ravine… The horse which remained in the roadway died soon after, the guard was found underneath the horse.

Most of the injured persons were removed to the Cottage Hospital, but several were accommodated at hotels and lodging-houses. Fourteen of the passengers sustained injuries which necessitated medical attendance…

Some of the passengers returned to Ilfracombe by steamer on Saturday. They expressed astonishment that the coach did not go over the precipice, and attribute the prevention of such a calamity to Colwill's presence of mind. All join in praising the driver for the manner in which he acted in the trying emergency.

North Devon Journal, 17 August 1893

The injuries were serious. Miss Jane Waugh, a milliner from Manchester, had multiple fractures and died a week later. Several other passengers had broken limbs and one had a fractured skull. Sam Colwill had suffered deep wounds to the head and leg when he plummeted into the ravine. Alfred Sollis, the guard, had had a carriage wheel roll over his stomach.

Who was responsible for the accident? An inquest jury decided that 'no blame was attached to the driver of the coach'. But what about the children who caused the horses to bolt? One passenger giving evidence at the inquest stated that he did not believe the children intended to frighten the horses. Privately the villagers were less certain. While some felt sure the youngsters acted innocently, others suspected they intended to make the horses bolt.

Sam Colwill eventually recovered from his physical injuries, but he had visibly aged and decided that the time had come to retire from the box seat. For almost 39 years he had driven coaches from Ilfracombe to Lynton. Now Sam gave that responsibility to his son, Tom, though he still ran the coaching business. Every

NOTICE TO THE PUBLIC.

— —

MRS. SAM COLWILL, MISS COLWILL, & MR. TOM COLWILL beg to return their most sincere Thanks to the large number of inquirers, respecting the accident to the Coach "Benita."

They also take this opportunity of thanking the many friends from a distance — letters having been received from all parts of the Kingdom — who have written so kindly of Mr. Sam Colwill, and expressing their deep regret at the injury to him, as well as to others.

It is with much satisfaction they are able to state that all the injured are progressing favourably, and the Colwill family extend to them their utmost sympathy.

Dated Coach Offices, 96, High-St., Ilfracombe, August 17th. 1893.

58:

A notice in the Ilfracombe Observer, *shortly after the tragic accident.*

Ilfracombe, 1894. Sam Colwill, photographed with his dog. He had retired after his accident in the previous year. His son, Tom, is driving the coach.

morning Sam would stand outside his Ilfracombe booking office to watch the departure of the *Benita*. What memories must have come flooding back of his coaching days on the Lynton road!

Hollerday House

AFTER THEIR first visit in 1887, George Newnes and his wife, Priscilla, returned each summer for a holiday and gradually fell in love with Lynton and Lynmouth. For several years they rented a gentleman's residence for their stay, but then they began to think seriously about having their own house built at the resort.

Lynton in 1871. Summit Castle, a lodging-house, is on the hill. Below it is the rectory (now Garson House) and on the left a farm building.

Rumours of a Mansion

Late in 1890 the news broke that George Newnes had purchased Hollerday Hill and intended to have a mansion erected there. Needless to say, local people were delighted:

It is rumoured that Mr Newnes M.P., has purchased a large part of Haliday Hill, also the glebe dairy farm and walled-in gardens abutting Lee Lane, altogether amounting to several acres, with the intention to erect on the summit a residence for himself. The house and grounds will command an extensive and magnificent land and water view, also the whole of the works of the Cliff Railway, the esplanade and the contemplated pier. The house is to be approached by a winding road, cut into the side of the hill from Lee Road, a lodge being placed at the entrance.

North Devon Journal, 9 October 1890

Making an Approach Road

The first task was to make a road to the proposed site. This was no easy task, for George Newnes loved horses and was determined to ensure they would not suffer unduly while pulling carriages up the hillside. Disregarding the cost, he gave instructions that the drive was to take a winding route and that in places the gradient was to be lessened by making a deep cutting in the hillside. Construction began in May 1891:

Work has been commenced in earnest by Messrs. Jones Bros. on the approach road to the site of Mr Newnes' mansion. It starts at a point directly opposite Miss Taylor's refreshment rooms, passing up the old road leading to Summit Castle House, which will be considerably widened and improved. It will then pass through the dairy farmyard and a field to the site for the mansion on the summit of Holliday Hill. In several places it will be cut to 20ft. in depth. To make the ascent as gradual as possible it will be made zig-zag.

North Devon Journal, 28 May 1891

An Unfortunate Accident

On Monday 13 July 1891 the excavations for the new road were briefly halted by an unfortunate accident:

At Lynton on Monday, about noon, one of Messrs. Jones Bros. butts was being laden with stone, at the new road now being made from Vicarage

The workmen who built Hollerday House.

Lane to Mr Newnes' property on Haliday Hill. To make this road, a cutting, some 30 feet deep, through hard rock, has to be made.

On the explosion of a mine, fired to loosen the stone, some of the flying debris struck the horse drawing the butt, and the animal immediately rushed off down the steep incline. Plunging against the pavement on the opposite side of Lee Lane, it came in contact with Brockington House refreshment rooms, completely demolishing the plate-glass windows, and breaking down the entrance door. The sudden jerk caused the stones in the butt to be pitched into the room, doing considerable damage to the furniture.

The horse then proceeded on its mad career by the Valley Hotel, over the Castle Hill and down Directions Hill, when it came into violent contact with the guard wall directly outside the Castle Lodge gates. The force of the collision broke the shafts, while the horse turned a somersault clean over the wall into a woody dell some 30 feet below. The unfortunate animal was fearfully cut about the body, and was speedily put out of its misery by two shots fired by Mr Widden.

North Devon Journal, 16 July 1891

Laying the Foundations

When George Newnes abandoned his pier scheme in February 1892 almost all building work was halted. It was even rumoured that Mr Newnes had given up the idea of having a mansion built, so in October the news that building work had actually begun on this major project was greeted with delight by those who hoped to obtain work there:

> The building of a mansion for Mr G.Newnes, M.P., on Holiday Hill, has just been commenced. The digging for the foundations is now almost completed, and it is intended to commence walling very shortly. The building, which will cost about £10,000, is wanted in about 8 months. Mr Bob Jones is the architect and builder. Great satisfaction is felt that the work has been undertaken by Messrs. Jones Bros. here, as it is believed that local workmen will be employed. This will be a boon to the workmen of Lynton and Lynmouth, as the building trade has been almost at a standstill of late, many workmen being compelled to leave the neighbourhood. Although Mr Newnes has been staying here during the summer, nothing more has been heard of the Pier and Harbour scheme.
>
> North Devon Journal, 13 October 1892

An Exposed Position

Difficulties were encountered when trying to work at such an elevated site in the winter months:

> The magnificent building being erected by Messrs. Jones Bros., on Holiday Hill for Mr Newnes, M.P., is being pushed ahead with all possible speed. Many difficulties, however, impede the progress of the work. The elevated position of the building exposes the work-

Hollerday House in 1907.

The Cliff Railway in Edwardian times. Hollerday House stands high on the hill.

men to 'every stormy wind that blows', while the huge blocks of freestone, as well as the native stone, have to be carefully prepared by the stone-cutters. But the building is steadily rising, and it is evident that it will be an ornament to the neighbourhood. The adjoining grounds have been planted with fir trees and evergreens.

North Devon Journal, 2 March 1893

An Ecstatic Welcome

The work of building the mansion was virtually complete by the end of 1893. George Newnes was made a baronet in the New Year's Honours List of 1895, and in the months that followed he successfully piloted the Lynton and Barnstaple Railway Bill through Parliament. Lyntonians dearly wanted a railway, so this won him back the popularity he had lost when he had changed his mind over his pier scheme. So when in July of that year Sir George and Lady Newnes arrived in Lynton for a holiday at their new mansion they received a rapturous welcome:

The Town Hall was given to the inhabitants by Sir George Newnes in 1900, to be used for their 'instruction and recreative pleasure'. From his mansion Sir George could look down on it.

Sir George and Lady Newnes were accorded a most enthusiastic reception on arriving at Lynton on Tuesday evening last. The carriage was met at Lynbridge by a large crowd of the inhabitants, consisting mainly of working-men. The horses were taken out of the carriage and the vehicle was drawn by hand in to Lynton and up to Sir George's magnificent mansion on Hollerday Hill. The procession was headed by the season band, which had been considerably augmented for the occasion. The town had been gaily decorated with flags. The streets were lined with people, who cheered heartily for Sir George and Lady Newnes as the procession passed.

On reaching the mansion Sir George said he felt overcome by the kindness they had shown him by giving himself and Lady Newnes such a hearty reception. He cordially thanked the inhabitants for this proof of their goodwill.

At 9.30 a torchlight procession was formed. After the streets of Lynton had been paraded, the residence of Sir George Newnes was visited… The hon. baronet said that he fell in love with Lynton on his first visit, and he felt a deeper interest in the place than ever, since he had come to live amongst them... The speech was received with cheers, and at the conclusion the band played, and the crowd sang, 'For he's a jolly good fellow', after which they left the mansion.

North Devon Journal, 1 August 1895

A Bowling Green

In 1905 Sir George purchased Summit Castle, an old lodging-house which blocked the view from his mansion. Its subsequent demolition provided the site for a new bowling green:

Although he is a busy man, Sir George Newnes, Bart., M.P., finds a little time for the fascinating and healthful game of bowls — being moreover a clever player. At Lynton he is doing his best to encourage a love of the old-time recreation among others.

Some months ago Lynton's benefactor acquired the property known as Summit Castle, and he practically passed it over to Mr Tom Jones, to

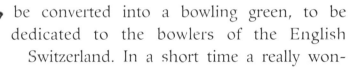

The member for Swansea. A cartoon, 1900.

be converted into a bowling green, to be dedicated to the bowlers of the English Switzerland. In a short time a really wonderful transformation has been effected, for the grounds of Summit Castle have been cleared of the old building... and a bowling green which is admired by everyone has been provided...

In the words of Sir George Newnes the green was 'christened' on Monday when (at Sir George's invitation) a team representing Victoria Park Bowling Club, Barnstaple, visited Lynton and played an exhibition game with local players. The visitors first sat down to a sumptuous lunch provided by Sir George Newnes at the Royal Castle Hotel.

Sir George Newnes, who had left Lynton a week earlier in his superb yacht the *Albion*, in order to pay his constituents a visit in Wales, was to have thrown the first ball in connection with the bowling match, but much to his regret the return of the *Albion* was delayed by bad weather…

The whole of the home members played pluckily, but it was Victoria's splendid combination that proved Lynton's undoing, the visitors winning by 222 to 58.

Sir George Newnes' yacht (which at Swansea has been visited by 25,000 people) was sighted about eighteen miles off about half-past-three o'clock… On the arrival of the *Albion* at Lynmouth, Sir George Newnes, accompanied by Lady Newnes and Miss Hillyard, their niece, at once came ashore in the motor launch; and not long afterwards the party put in an appearance at the bowling green and watched the game with considerable interest.

North Devon Journal, 14 September 1905

Mourning

Sadly, George Newnes' health began to fail in the summer of 1909. He and his wife took up permanent residence at Hollerday House and it was there that he died in June 1910, at the age of fifty-nine:

It is with profound regret that we have to record the death of Sir George Newnes, Bart., who passed away on Thursday morning at his beautiful residence on Hollerday Hill, Lynton. The deceased gentleman, who had for some time suffered from diabetes, was taken seriously ill while at Lynton eight weeks ago, and although he rallied, complications which set

Sir George Newnes, towards the end of his life.

in precluded all hope of his ultimate recovery. Lady Newnes, his devoted wife, and Mr Frank Newnes, his only son, were present when he breathed his last. For many years Sir George had filled a commanding place in the life of Lynton, and the news of his decease was received with the deepest sorrow by all classes of the community.

North Devon Journal, 16 June 1910

Fire

After the funeral, Frank Newnes, Sir George's son, discovered that most of his late father's fortune had gone and the family had been left with unpaid debts. Lady Newnes and Frank decided to shut Hollerday House and leave Lynton. The furniture was sold at auction and the mansion was put up for sale. It stood empty, for no one would meet the asking price. Then, at eleven o'clock on the night of 4 August 1913, fire broke out:

The placid calm which usually distinguishes Lynton, even at the height of the holiday season, was rudely disturbed on Monday night, when Hollerday House was totally destroyed by fire...

The fire at Hollerday House, 4 August 1913.

That Hollerday House was deliberately set on fire on Monday night not the slightest doubt is entertained, and there is strong suspicion that the crime was the work of Suffragists. The mansion having been unoccupied and unfurnished for some time, no fires had been lit in any of the rooms for some months. A most suspicious circumstance is that almost simultaneously with the alarm on Monday night fires were raging in two distinct parts of the house, whilst — although on this point opinion differs — many persons insist that during the progress of the fire there were violent explosions, this suggesting that highly combustible substances had previously been placed in the mansion in order to aid the work of destruction...

Inspecting the interior of Hollerday House on the morning after the fire.

It was 11.10 p.m. to the minute on Monday when the first alarm of the outbreak was given. At that time P.C. Sparkes was in the square at Lynton. Hearing a woman shout nearby, he looked up and at once saw that Hollerday House was on fire. The constable sent a man to call ex-constable Bibbings, who promptly summoned the Fire Brigade, and meanwhile hastened up to Hollerday...

The Fire Brigade (under Capt. Long) were on the spot with their hose reel with commendable promptitude. The hall door had to be forced, and the hose was immediately directed on the massive oaken staircase and the tower end, where the fire was now raging fiercely. Hollerday is supplied with water pumped up from the Company's mains near the Town Hall, a large tank at the back being always kept full. The pressure from the mains is quite sufficient to send a jet of water over the highest buildings in the town, but Hollerday being situated at an exceptional height, the firemen found themselves at a disadvantage, so far as the supply of water was concerned.

It was at once evident that to save the main building was an impossibility, but with the single length of hose at their disposal, and the supply of water available, the Brigade did marvellously well. As time went on, floor on floor collapsed in the mansion, the flames rising to a tremendous height, and the noise at times caused by falling timber and masonry was deafening. The heat was terrific, and at some points the workers could not approach the fire within a distance of fifty feet. Finally, the remaining portions of the roof collapsed, the huge conflagration not being brought under complete control until about 2 a.m.

When all was over Hollerday House (or to be precise, its remains) presented a weird spectacle. Looked at from Station Hill, the front of the ivy-clad mansion looks practically intact, but from Countisbury Hill side daylight shows through bare lines of gaunt walls… By a strange coincidence, the only sections of the mansion left standing are the morning room (a favourite apartment of Sir George Newnes, in which the late baronet breathed his last) and the billiard room.

North Devon Journal, 7 August 1913

The fire occurred at the height of the Suffragette demonstrations, so it was easy to blame the women who were campaigning for the vote. Yet when the police searched the smouldering ruins they found not even a hairpin to support the theory. So, if, as the evidence suggests, it was arson, who set fire to the house? This is a mystery which has still to be solved.

The ruins stood in splendid isolation until April 1933, when the Hollerday Hill estate was purchased by Mr John Holman and made over as a gift to the people of Lynton and Lynmouth. The remains of the building became a favourite play area

The ruins stood on Hollerday Hill for many years.

for local children, and then during World War Two were used as a training ground by the local Civil Defence. After the war it was decided the building had become dangerous and it was blown up as an exercise by the men of 42 Commando, Bickleigh. Now only a pile of rubble, overgrown with vegetation, marks the spot where a great man once lived.

Cutting The First Sod

ON THE morning of 17 September 1895, Lyntonians were in a state of high excitement. Sir George Newnes had recently obtained an Act of Parliament to build a railway from Barnstaple to Lynton, and on this momentous day the ceremony of cutting the first sod was to be performed. The day had been declared a public holiday; the inhabitants massed in the streets to watch Sir George and Lady Newnes, accompanied by the other railway directors, invited guests, bands,

The procession through Lynton prior to the cutting of the first sod, 17 September 1895.

The ceremony took place in a field where the railway station was to be built.

coastguards, members of the friendly societies in full regalia, councillors, and school children, move in procession through Lynton before making their way to the site chosen for the new station:

> Never in the whole of their history have the townships been decorated so freely and so gaily as on Tuesday. There were a large number of triumphal arches, whilst fir trees were planted along the principal streets, and flags, banners, fairy lamps and Chinese lanterns were suspended across the thoroughfares and displayed from the upper windows of the houses by the thousand...
>
> The proceedings of the day commenced at eleven o'clock, when there was a most imposing procession... The principal thoroughfares having been paraded, those taking part in the procession walked to a field called Shambleway Head, the scene of the projected terminus, where the

Lady Newnes is about to use a silver spade to cut the first sod. Sir George Newnes is the bearded man on her right.

ceremony was to take place. In glorious weather and before a crowd of several hundreds of persons... Lady Newnes then proceeded to perform the ceremony, lifting by means of a silver spade the first sod, depositing it in a magnificently carved oak barrow with silver mountings, then wheeling it to the end of a platform covered with crimson cloth, over-turning it, and finally returning with the barrow to the starting point

Sir George Newnes said his wife had asked him to return thanks for the kind way in which they had watched her difficult function that day. She had done her job in such a workmanlike fashion that he hoped the directors would give her regular employment in the construction of the railway. (Laughter.) This was in his judgement a great day for Lynton, Lynmouth, and for the district. (Applause.)

The interesting proceedings terminated with a hearty rendering of the

Lynton Station, c.1908.

National Anthem. Afterwards the procession was reformed, the principal thoroughfares being again paraded.

At half-past one o'clock there was a luncheon at the Valley of Rocks Hotel, Sir George Newnes presided over a very large gathering...

At two o'clock 400 men were entertained to dinner in Mr Moore's Floral Hall, whilst later on several hundreds of women and children sat down to tea in the same building, all enjoying themselves thoroughly...

In the evening the well-known firm of Pain and Sons, London, gave a grand firework display on Hollerday Hill. Sir George Newnes' mansion presented a charming appearance, being brilliantly illuminated with nearly 4,000 Chinese lanterns and fairy lights. The surrounding grounds also looked resplendent with fairy lights and coloured lanterns. The fireworks concluded with a magnificent representation of an engine, and the words 'Success to the Lynton and Barnstaple Railway'. A number of rockets from Sir George Newnes' yacht were let off during the evening. At 9.30 a torchlit procession, headed by the Season Band, paraded the streets of Lynton, and marched to Sir G.Newnes' mansion, from the balcony of which the hon. baronet addressed the assembled crowd. Large bonfires were lighted on the surrounding hills... The scene was very brilliant, and the illuminations eclipsed anything previously seen at Lynton.

North Devon Journal, 19 September 1895

The construction of the Lynton and Barnstaple Railway was delayed by disputes with local landowners and by practical problems caused by the hilly terrain. The line finally opened on 11 May 1898 amid rejoicing. Yet not all the locals celebrated: coachmen, grooms and blacksmiths watched with dismay as the Barnstaple four-horse coach set off for the last time.

Developments At Woody Bay

THREE MILES west of Lynton is Woody Bay, a long sweep of the coast where twisted old oaks spread down steep cliffs towards the rocky shore. Yet this remote bay might well have been developed into a busy holiday resort rivalling Lynton and Lynmouth, if the plans of Colonel Benjamin Lake had come to fruition.

This wealthy solicitor from Orpington in Kent bought the manor of Martinhoe

Making a new road near the Glen Hotel, Woody Bay, 1896.

Carriage approaching the road from Woody Bay to Hunter's Inn, c.1900. Colonel Lake built this as a carriage road, but it is now a coastal footpath.

in 1885 and included in the estate was Woody Bay, then sometimes known as Wooda Bay. Soon he announced ambitious plans to create an exclusive resort there. Martinhoe Manor House was converted into a hotel (then known as the Wooda Bay Hotel). He built the Glen Hotel (now called the Woody Bay Hotel) and leased it out. In May 1894 Colonel Lake opened a new golf course on Martinhoe Common. He also sold off plots along the wooded slopes for development, and it was not long before a few large villas began to peep out through the trees.

The Glen Hotel (now the Woody Bay Hotel), c.1895.

Lake came to realise that his plans were doomed to failure unless he could make Woody Bay more accessible from the outside world. So between 1893 and 1895 he had new roads made to the bay. When the Lynton and Barnstaple Railway was proposed in 1895, Lake gave permission for the line to cross his land on advantageous terms, on condition that a station was built at the point where the railway would come closest to the bay.

Colonel Lake also cast covetous eyes on the many holiday-makers using the Bristol Channel steamers. He felt sure that sea access was a key to success, but could the steamers be persuaded to call at Woody Bay? The answer, he decided, was to build a pier. Work started late in 1895.

Great Expectations

In October 1895 a *North Devon Journal* reporter wrote an enthusiastic report about Woody Bay's prospects:

> Woody Bay is destined to attain fame as a watering place in the not far-distant future...

Building Woody Bay Pier, 28 February 1896.

(left): The workmen who built Woody Bay Pier, 15 April 1896. (below): A diver inspecting the piles, 31 July 1896.

The splendidly-constructed new cliff road to Woody Bay, may be said to form the first portion of the scheme for developing the estate. Starting from the Hunter's Inn, the road is three miles in length, and gradually rises to a height of 700 feet… Over the Woody Bay Drive, for such is the name of the road, there has already been considerable coaching traffic, and visitors making excursions from Ilfracombe, Lynton, and other places express themselves as being wonderfully pleased with it. The new road connects with the old road at Woody Bay, and also leads to Martinhoe Common, which is less than one mile distant. Here, land

Workmen on the pier, 21 January 1897. Notice the steep approach road and steps down to the pier.

having been reclaimed and seeded out, golf links have already been established, which visitors say are very good...

A mile further on is Woolhanger Cross, which, about two miles from Woody Bay, will form the *locale* for a station of the Lynton and Barnstaple Railway...

There are at present two hotels, by name 'Woody Bay' and 'Glen-Lyn', together with five other lodging-houses, which are in the cottage-villa style, with red-tile roofs...

The pier will be constructed of creosoted pitch-pine piles, which are encased up to low-water mark in wrought-iron cylinders, the intervening space being filled in with concrete...

A great deal will soon be heard of Woody Bay and the locality. There is a brilliant future in store for the delightful spot.

North Devon Journal, 10 October 1895

The article painted a rosy picture, but in fact Colonel Lake was already encountering major difficulties. He was having to find more and more money to fund his grandiose plans.

Hunter's Inn in 1890.

Fire at Hunter's Inn

Colonel Lake soon had another problem to face. Included in his purchase of the manor of Martinhoe in 1885 had been Hunter's Inn, in the Heddon Valley. One windy afternoon in November 1895 the thatch at this attractive inn caught fire and the building was gutted. His tenant, Mr Berry, was only partly insured:

> The news that the quaint, picturesque Hunter's Inn was on Saturday afternoon entirely destroyed by fire will be read with widespread regret. How the fire originated is not quite certain, but it is supposed to have

The remains of Hunter's Inn, 10 January 1896. Fire had gutted the inn.

Workmen rebuilding Hunter's Inn, 25 May 1897.

The rebuilt Hunter's Inn, 24 July 1900.

been due to some defect in a chimney. Unfortunately only Mrs and the Misses Berry (3) were at home at the time of the outbreak, Mr Berry, with his sons and men, being engaged on a farm at Cherryford.

About three o'clock, when postman James Tamlyn arrived, Miss Annie Berry observed smoke issuing from the top of the house. Investigation showed that the thatch roof was on fire. Tamlyn did all that he could, and then went for assistance, but with a strong wind blowing up the valley the place was gutted ere the ready help came.

North Devon Journal, 28 November 1895

Colonel Lake had to bear most of the cost of rebuilding the inn. His purse seemed bottomless, for he erected an imposing hotel which looked not unlike a Swiss chalet.

Lee Abbey, early in the 20th century.

Bottom Lodge, Lee Abbey, early 20th century. The road was private beyond the gate.

Top Lodge, Lee Abbey, early 20th century.

By January 1897 Lake's pier was virtually complete and there was consternation in Lynton and Lynmouth when the Campbell Steamer Company announced that in future its vessels would call at Woody Bay instead of at Lynmouth, which still lacked good landing facilities. The company suggested that steamer passengers wishing to visit Lynton and Lynmouth could be taken there in coaches from Woody Bay pier. This idea was virtually ruled out when Charles Bailey, the owner of Lee Abbey, made it clear that he would not allow coach loads of excursionists to pass through his estate on their way from Woody Bay to the twin villages.

The Lynton and Lynmouth tradespeople were distraught at the prospect of losing their sea-borne visitors. Fortunately for Lynmouth, the Campbell Steamer Company soon withdrew its threat to cease calling there. Probably the company realised that very few passengers would want to visit Woody Bay, and there would be problems landing those who did.

An Unfortunate Opening

The biggest drawback with the Woody Bay pier was that it did not stretch far enough out into the sea to allow for the large tidal range. This meant vessels could not berth there at low water. One writer described how tide and weather conspired to ruin its official opening on 15 April 1897:

The opening of the pier, 15 April 1897. The event was a fiasco, for the tide was out and the steamer could not come alongside the pier.

I was staying at the hotel at the time and well do I remember the opening. It was a real Devonshire day of continuous driving rain. The steamer arrived off the pier, but, as this was not long enough, was not able to come alongside, and two wretched pressmen were landed in a small boat.

Will Sherracombe, Devon Exmoor (1928)

Rumours of New Projects

It soon became clear that very few steamers were calling at Woody Bay. Lake's response was to have plans drawn up for a big extension to his pier. There were also rumours of much more ambitious schemes:

Since Woody Bay pier has opened it has become apparent that it is not perfect, so that steamers from Bristol can come alongside at all stages of the tide and land passengers comfortably. This was brought to the notice of Colonel Lake, the owner, who at once gave instructions for the pier to be lengthened, so as to take passengers at all stages of the tide. The work will cost about £4,000. It is proposed to build an open pier commencing near the northern end of the existing pier and extending seawards in a north-easterly direction for about 150 feet, and thence north-north-westerly for nearly 100 feet.

It is further hinted that Colonel Lake intends to provide a lift, as at Lynmouth, and connect it with a line to the Woolhanger Cross station of the new Lynton and Barnstaple railway. This is quite in the order of things, bearing in mind the splendid enterprise which Colonel Lake has shown in developing this very beautiful corner of North Devon.

Woody Bay pier, 1897. The steep descent to the pier was a big disadvantage.

(Above): Passengers waiting on the pier to board a steamer on a wet day, c.1898. (Left): A steamer calls at the pier, 1897.

A lift and a connection with the railway would enable steamer passengers to travel to Barnstaple, Bideford, Westward Ho!, Clovelly and other places in that direction in a very enjoyable way…

It is quite time Lynmouth itself woke up, and provided a pier near the new esplanade, so that passengers by steamer could alight in a more comfortable way than by the present inconvenient boats.

Lynton and Lynmouth Recorder, 15 August 1898

The pier was never extended, for financial problems were crowding in on Lake. Yet still he went on spending money. In 1899 work began to build the Station Hotel facing Woody Bay Station.

Woody Bay Station, early 20th century. The Station Hotel can be seen beyond the station.

The Station Hotel, near Woody Bay Station, in the 1920s.

Disaster Strikes

Early in July 1900, the newspapers carried sensational news. Colonel Lake was bankrupt! At the London Bankruptcy Court that October it was revealed he had debts of over £170,000. The following week he was arrested and charged with misappropriating money invested with him in his capacity as a solicitor. It was claimed he had been using his clients' savings to pay for his development of Woody Bay, and to fund reckless speculation in Kent coal mining shares. In January 1901 he was tried at the Old Bailey and was sentenced to twelve years in prison. He died in 1909, a broken man. His is a tragic story.

Sale of the Estate

The Woody Bay estate had to be sold to pay off some of the colonel's debts. The following newspaper report shows that Woody Bay was still thought to have the potential to be developed into a successful resort:

> The most important property sale which has taken place in North Devon for many years was that at the Royal and Fortescue Hotel, Barnstaple, on Tuesday, of the well-known Wooda Bay Estate, near Lynton, which came into the market by reason of the sensational failure of the owner, Col. Benjamin Greene Lake, solicitor of London, and J.P. of Devon.
>
> A handsome illustrated catalogue published by the vendors described the estate as... 'a charming building property comprising many unrivalled sites for the erection of family mansions, marine villa residences, shops and private hotels... A considerable outlay has been already made on the property and the whole is ripe for further development, either as a popular pleasure resort, or for the erection of high-class residences'.
>
> North Devon Journal, 18 October 1900

In the event most of the estate was purchased by Charles Bailey, the owner of the adjacent Lee Abbey estate. He had no wish to see Woody Bay being transformed into a holiday resort and he at once put an end to all development.

* * * * *

The Woody Bay pier itself came to a sad end. It had been in use for less than two years when it was severely damaged in the great gale of 12 January 1899. Some have suggested that a group of local people, opposed to the development of the bay, may have sabotaged the structure. It is possible, but the only evidence which might support the theory is that most of the initial damage occurred in the section nearest to the pier-head. Further damage was caused by gales in the following

The damaged pier, 1901.

Demolition of the pier in progress, 11 June 1902. Most of the work had to be done by boat.

winter. In June 1902 work began to demolish the remaining sections, and the salvaged materials were then sold for scrap.

A vessel towing away salvaged materials, 11 June 1902.

Remains of the pier can still be seen today. The concrete pier-head is still there. On the beach are to be found a few traces of the pitch-pine posts which for a few brief years supported the pier. They survive as reminders of an ill-judged scheme. Perhaps we should rejoice that Colonel Lake's efforts to create a holiday resort failed, for today we can still enjoy the haunting beauty and tranquil solitude which make Woody Bay so very special.

Day-Trippers

FIVE TIMES in the late nineteenth century Parliamentary powers were obtained to build a landing pier at Lynmouth and five times the schemes were abandoned, partly on cost grounds, but mainly due to opposition from wealthy residents. This influential group tolerated the relatively small numbers of day-trippers ferried ashore in boats from the steamers, but viewed with dread the prospect of hundreds or even thousands of excursionists landing at a pier and spending the day in the resort.

After the opening of the Lynton and Barnstaple Railway in 1898, Lynmouth tradespeople became convinced they were losing business to Lynton, which was easier to reach from the new station. So in 1901 they launched yet another campaign to try and obtain a pier.

Landing at Lynmouth, 1908. Passengers were ferried ashore from the steamers in small boats. When the tide was out they had to scramble over the stony beach.

The Lynton Cottage, c.1880. This was a private hotel entertaining wealthy visitors.

Opposition to a Pier

Wealthy residents and long-stay visitors wrote letters to the local press warning that they would desert the resort if a pier was built. Most of the Lynton hoteliers were also opposed to a pier, for they feared they would lose many of their affluent customers if there was an influx of day-trippers. The *North Devon Herald* shared their concern:

> Numerous residents in the charming North Devon resort object to their quiet little haven being over-run by cheap and nasty tourists who, whilst spending little or nothing themselves of any consequence to the shopkeepers and hotel proprietors of the place, successfully drive away the money-spending community in the form of season visitors and resident householders...
>
> The class of individual carried by the cheap excursion steamers seldom expends very much money at refreshment-rooms, tea rooms and

Lynmouth Harbour in Edwardian times. Visitors appreciated the sedate pace of life.

hotels, although the public houses and shooting galleries may perhaps pick up stray coppers here and there...

If they prefer the noisy patronage of Dick, Tom and 'Arry with their concertinas and mouth organs to the annual and sometimes uninterrupted visits of refined and wealthy families with biggish accounts at the local tradesmen's establishments, and profitable business orders for hotel proprietors, bait stables and other providers, then there is nothing more to be said. In this case let the pier go ahead without delay and let Lynmouth vie with Margate, Ramsgate, Bournemouth and Weymouth for the pence and the impudence of the holiday tripper: but at the same time let it make up its mind to forego the fat cheques and the crisp banknotes of the better-class families.

North Devon Herald, 13 June 1901

Outside the Lyndale Hotel, c.1907. Lynmouth was still a genteel resort. It escaped the large influxes of trippers experienced by Ilfracombe, which had a landing pier.

Support for a Pier

The *North Devon Journal* took the opposite view to its rival. Later in the same month it put forward the case for improved landing facilities at Lynmouth:

> The arguments in favour of the construction of a pier at Lynmouth are absolutely unanswerable. During the season it frequently happens that excursionists by steamer for Lynmouth are unable to land. The veriest tyro must be able to see how such a state of things is likely to prejudice a watering place. Can Lynton and Lynmouth afford to ignore the possibility of patronage that the tapping of the steamer traffic that passes this lovely coast presents? This is the crucial question. And there is no doubt as to

what the answer of the bulk of the persons concerned with the prosperity of the twin villages would be.

The only argument seriously argued against the erection of a pier is that it would tend to 'vulgarise' the district by introducing the 'tripper' element. But such an argument is wholly out of date. According to this theory it would have been better for Lynton to have stuck to the old coach service.

The contempt which some people pour on the unfortunate tripper is, however, the outcome of pure snobbery. As if a man who can only afford a day's holiday is not as much entitled to the enjoyment of the country's beauty spots as the superior being whose holiday is merely governed by inclination! The assumption that only undesirables would come by steamer is an insult.

North Devon Journal, 27 June 1901

Another Warning

In the same week the *North Devon Herald* again warned of the serious implications if a pier was to be built:

It may be taken for granted that all the Punch and Judy shows, shooting galleries, Aunt Sallies, switchbacks etc which choose to come and pay their footing will be welcome. And come they will as sure as night follows day. These are precisely the amusements which tickle the imagination of the delectable passengers who will be brought in their hundreds and thousands by the excursion steamers from Bristol, Newport, Cardiff, Penarth and Barry and upon whom the Pier Company will rely to make their venture pay…

None of the gentlemen who have come year after year to Lynmouth on account of its special recommendations for quiet and repose will repeat their experience when once Lynmouth has become a 'popular' watering place. It cannot be both a residential and an excursion centre. It must irrevocably choose between the two.

North Devon Herald, 27 June 1901

The opponents of a pier once again won the day. While some of the Lynmouth tradespeople were extremely vocal, it became clear that most of the influential people with money to spend dreaded the prospect of an influx of day-trippers. It proved impossible to find a promoter who would risk his money seeking Parliamentary approval for a pier, and the campaign soon fizzled out.

Lynton and Lynmouth had chosen to remain a small, picturesque resort catering mainly for long-stay visitors, rather than trying to become a commercialised resort attracting large numbers of day-trippers.

The Coming of the Motor Coach

One of the earliest motor cars to appear in Lynton has stopped near Directions Corner, perhaps in need of assistance.

An Early Motor-Coach Service

IN 1903 George Newnes, the Chairman of the Lynton and Barnstaple Railway Company, decided to set up a company to operate motor-buses between Ilfracombe and Blackmoor Gate, as a feeder service for the railway. He had been concerned to see that most people travelling between Ilfracombe and Lynton still did all the journey by horse-drawn coach, instead of transferring to the train at Blackmoor Gate. He hoped that motor coaches would prove a novel attraction and would attract many passengers who would then finish their journey to Lynton on the train. This was an experiment way ahead of its time, for motor vehicles were still in their infancy. The arrival of two motor-buses in North Devon caused quite a stir:

There was much speculation as to the destination of two motor breaks which passed through Barnstaple on Thursday. Inquiry elicited the information that the motors are intended for the tourist traffic between Ilfracombe and Blackmoor Station. At the recent annual meeting of the Lynton and Barnstaple Railway Company Sir George Newnes, Bart., M. P., announced that, with a view to securing for the railway a larger share of the tourist traffic between Ilfracombe and Lynton, a motor service to Blackmoor had been arranged, and the hon. baronet expressed the opinion that the combined motor and train journey would prove very popular.

There can be no doubt that the new motor breaks will prove formidable rivals to the coaches which have for many seasons been in such great demand at Ilfracombe for the popular trip to Lynton. The new service will be more expeditious, and it will, we believe, be cheaper. Love of novelty will, too, operate in favour of the departure. The prevailing opinion is that the Lynton Railway Company has done a good stroke of business. The motor breaks are of 16 horse-power each and each car will accommodate 20 passengers (18 in the body of the vehicle, and two alongside the driver). The cars are covered, curtains being provided for use in bad weather. The makers are Milner, Daimler, Ltd., of London, and the cars belong to the Ilfracombe Motor Co.

North Devon Journal, 28 May 1903

Outside the Valley of Rocks Hotel, c.1920. Times are changing, visitors now arrive by motor vehicle.

The motor-coach service began on Saturday, 30 May. Passengers left Ilfracombe at 10.00 a.m., changed to the train at Blackmoor Gate and arrived at Lynton Station at 12.14 p.m. Unfortunately, the new motor coaches soon ran foul of the law. On 26 June two police officers timed one of them and claimed it was travelling at a 'furious rate… of 14 miles, 5 furlongs and 16 poles an hour'. The result was that the unfortunate driver appeared in court for what was a very early speeding case:

An interesting case was heard before the Combe Martin County Magistrates on Monday, in which Harry Jenner, the driver of the motor 'bus between Ilfracombe and Blackmoor Station, on the Lynton and Barnstaple Railway, and in the employ of the Ilfracombe Motor Coach Company, was summoned for driving the motor 'bus, 'the weight of which unladen is one ton and a half and does not exceed two tons', at a greater speed than eight miles per hour, contrary to the regulations with

Advertisement in the Ilfracombe Gazette, *3 July 1903, for the pioneer motor coach service which was to connect with the train at Blackmoor Gate.*

respect to the use of light locomotives on highways made by the Local Government Board.

The police stated that a distance was measured of one mile, two furlongs, and twenty-four poles in Long-lane, an unfrequented road between Berry Down and Easterclose Chapel, which is the junction with the main road between Combe Martin and Lynton. On June 26th defendant drove his 'bus over the measured distance in 5 min. 25 sec. according to the times taken by ordinary watches.

Mr Ffinch, who defended, addressed the Magistrates, pointing out that ample time was allowed for the journey of 11 miles, which was scheduled and performed in one hour and a half.

The Ilfracombe Motor Coach Co., Ltd.

ILFRACOMBE to LYNTON

By MOTOR COACH.

Ilfracombe to Blackmoor Gate, thence by L. & B. Narrow Gauge Line to Lynton.

EVERY WEEK DAY

UNTIL FURTHER NOTICE.

The Company's Cars will run a Daily Service as under:—

From Ilfracombe to Lynton

Leaving Ilfracombe, No. 119, High Street (opposite Town Hall, 10 a.m., arriving at Lynton 12-14 p.m.

Passengers return from Lynton (L. & B. Railway Station), at 4-10 p.m., arriving Ilfracombe, High Street, 6-30 p.m.

From Lynton to Ilfracombe

Leaving Lynton (L. & B. Railway Station), at 12-20 p.m., arriving Ilfracombe, High Street, at 2 p.m.

Passengers return from Ilfracombe, No. 119, High Street, at 3-45 p.m.

FARES (to and from Lynton): SINGLE, 3/-; RETURN, 4/-

☞ Seats may be booked at Mr. J. Delve's, Confectioner, 119, High Street, Ilfracombe.

At Lynton Tickets may be obtained at L. & B. Railway Station, or Mr. Tom Jones' Office, Church Hill House.

CHAS. E. DREWETT (Secretary),
The Ilfracombe Motor Coach Co., Ltd.,
21 & 22, Church Street, Ilfracombe.

Registered Offices— Pilton Bridge, Barnstaple.

Defendant admitted that his 'bus, or car, was travelling between 10 or 12 miles an hour over this portion of the road, which was unfrequented, and also had a sharp falling gradient.

Prideaux's Car-hire Depot, Lee Road, Lynton, c.1920. It was located next to the hospital.

> The Magistrates announced that the defendant would be fined £3 and costs for having exceeded eight miles per hour. The Chairman (Mr Clogg) stated that, as this was the first case, the fine had been lower than it otherwise would have been.
>
> North Devon Journal, 9 July 1903

George Newnes was disgusted with the treatment his pioneering motor-coach company had received. Early in July the closure of the bus service was announced. The vehicles were sold off to the Great Western Railway and this company used them on its first bus service between the Lizard and Helston Station.

The Demise of the Horse-Drawn Coach

Only a few more years elapsed before motor buses returned to the North Devon roads and began to take over from horse-drawn coaches. Colwills' four-horse

A horse-drawn coach, c.1920. An AA sign is a symbol of a newer form of transport

The Lynton to Minehead coach descending Porlock Hill just after World War One.

Coach leaving the Lyndale Hotel, c.1900. The success of Lorna Doone *had attracted many American visitors to the area and this is perhaps why the American flag is flying.*

Digging out the Minehead to Lynton motor coach on the road between Porlock and Lynmouth, April 1922. A blizzard on 1 April had halted all forms of transport.

coach ran between Ilfracombe and Lynton for the last time on 1 October 1910 and in the following season a motor charabanc was used on the service. The Lynton to Minehead horse-drawn coach service lasted longer, because early motor buses were unable to climb and safely descend the steep hills between the two resorts. Right up until the end of the 1919 season the departure of the Minehead coach was a highlight of the day at both Lynton and Lynmouth. In March 1920 came the sad announcement:

The ubiquitous motor bus has, as was inevitable, driven the grand, superbly-horsed Lynton, Lynmouth and Minehead coach off the road at

Motor coaches and cars outside St Mary's Church, 1929.

The last days of the horse-drawn coach. An excursion coach passes a garage belonging to the Lyn Valley Hotel as it sets off on the road to Watersmeet.

last. The pride of North Devon and West Somerset, its departure is viewed with the deepest regret by a huge number of visitors, and the residents along its route.

At Lynmouth and Minehead its arrival and departure were the events of the day, and in the intervening villages its passing was viewed with interest, the horn bringing every good housewife to the door. But in these utilitarian times sentiment must give way, people are in a hurry, in holiday keeping as in business. The three hours and a half coach journey is to be superseded by that of the motor taking little over half the time.

The old-time vehicle, after running for nearly eighty years, at first from Bridgwater, then Taunton, and latterly from Minehead as the G.W.R. travelled westwards, has now ceased, and travelling in the Exmoor country is 'up-to-date'. But the 'up-to-datedness' will not enable one to

Glen Lyn Garage, Lynmouth, opened c.1928.

so thoroughly appreciate this magnificent moorland drive as the old-time mode of travel. High up on the roof of *Lorna Doone* and *Red Deer* one had full views, keen health-giving moorland air, and time to enjoy the beauty rolling away on either side of one to the horizon of sea or mountain. The new vehicles retain the old names, and will be speedy and comfortable.

North Devon Journal, 11 March 1920

Times were changing. Horse-drawn coach excursions still ran for a few more years from Lynton to the Doone Valley and other local beauty spots. Yet even on those routes the motor coach eventually took over. The horse-drawn coaches had been a special feature of holidays at Lynton and Lynmouth, but their day was done. The motor coach had come to stay.

The Lynrock Mineral-Water Company

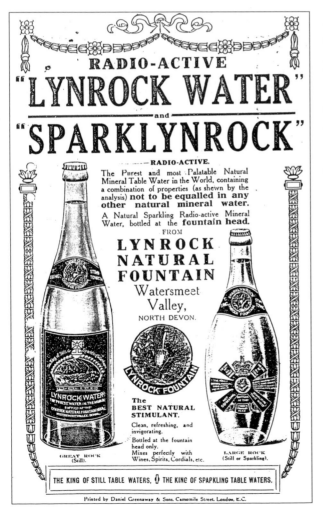

A MILE upstream from Lynmouth on the East Lyn, a natural spring emerges from the base of the valley side. By 1911 the Lynrock Mineral-Water Company had been set up to exploit this natural resource.

The Bottling Process

The water was bottled in a small building known as the 'Lynrock Mineral-Water Factory', which was situated next to the spring. The machines in this bottling plant were at first driven by hydraulic ram, and later by a small hydro-electric generator, operated by water taken from further upstream.

From the start the company made extravagant claims. An early advertisement declared:

An advertisement for Lynrock mineral water, c.1912. It made some surprising claims.

The Lynrock Mineral-Water Factory in the East Lyn Valley, c.1912.

The utmost care is taken to insure absolute cleanliness, and the exclusion of atmospheric air, during the process of filling and capsuling by the most improved machinery and methods.

The water passes direct from the rock through a silver pipe to a white marble glass-covered tank; from this tank it is conducted through silver-lined pipes to the silver-lined filling chambers of the Still, and Sparkling, Bottling and Capsuling Machines.

This process excludes all handling until the bottles have been capsuled, which is done by the most improved machine, ensuring an absolute air and gas-tight sealing.

Advertisement, c.1912

Radioactive Water!

The Lynrock Mineral-Water Company boasted that its water was the 'purest in the world'. Perhaps more surprising was the claim that its water was 'radioactive', implying that this made it an invaluable cure-all:

Lynrock Fountain. Here the spring water could be sampled.

WHAT IS CLAIMED FOR 'LYNROCK WATER'

THAT it is the king of radio-active British drinking waters, unequalled for quality by any foreign water.

THAT unlike other mineral waters, it does not depress the system, but acts as an invigorating tonic.

THAT an equal combination of properties, as shown by the analysis, is not to be found in any other natural mineral water, and that these properties mark it out for the treatment of the following complaints: gout, rheumatism, liver complaints, kidney disease, dyspepsia, anaemia, blood and skin impurities, constipation.

A Free Sample

A stop at the Lynrock Mineral-Water Factory was a real highlight for visitors walking up the valley to Watersmeet on a hot summer day. Under a shelter, next to the main building, was a spring where the water could be sampled. The water came pouring out of the rock through a chrome pipe, and a mug, chained to a wall, was provided for the public to use. A guidebook advised:

> Just before Myrtleberry, and on the same side, is a spring of absolutely pure water. The visitor can now cross by a neat wooden bridge, and, resting, in a small chalet, drink his glass of 'Lyn Rock' water, which is said to contain valuable medicinal properties.
>
> Ward Lock Guide to Lynton and Lynmouth (c.1920)

"THE KING OF TABLE WATERS."

Unlike other Mineral Waters, **does not depress the System,** but acts as an **Invigorating Tonic.**

Highly Recommended by Medical Authorities for the treatment of **Gout, Rheumatism, Acidity, Indigestion** (Chronic and Acute), **Anæmia, Blood Impurities, Liver Complaints, Kidney Diseases, Constipation and Neuritis.**

Soft Drinks

For many years the Lynrock Mineral-Water Company was run by members of the Attree family who lived at Myrtleberry, just upstream from the spring. The Ford Model T open truck they used to distribute their bottled water became a familiar sight on local roads. They also began to supply lemonade and other soft drinks as the following newspaper advertisement shows:

A GENUINE bank note has a water mark. Lynton also has a water mark which is 'Lynton Natural Mineral Water', the king of table waters and the purest in the world. Bottled at the famous Lyn Rock spring, situated in the

A postcard advertising Lynrock mineral water.

Watersmeet Valley, Lynmouth. Aerated also *en* Soda, Lemonade, Ginger-beer and Ginger Ale. Unequalled in quality or purity by any other mineral waters on the market — Proprietors, Attree Bros., Lyn Rock Offices, Lynmouth.

North Devon Journal, 18 March 1920

The bottling plant flourished through the 1920s, but then sales began to decline and it finally closed shortly before World War Two. The building was swept away in the flood of 15 August 1952. All that survives today are remnants of the rear walls, and the mineral spring itself, now marked by a plaque.

The First Months
of War

ON 4 AUGUST 1914 German troops invaded Belgium and began marching towards France. The British government sent an ultimatum demanding an immediate withdrawal. There was no response. Britain therefore declared war on Germany. A great European tragedy had been set in motion. Lynton and Lynmouth seemed remote from the battlefields, but the resort could not escape the consequences of the epic struggle taking place on the Continent.

The members of the Lynton and Lynmouth Territorial Army unit were soon mobilised. These young part-time soldiers had signed up in peace time, attracted no doubt by the lure of a two-week summer camp, in an age when few working lads had the chance to go away on holiday. In 1910 they had proudly attended the opening of the Valley of Rocks gun shed (since converted into Cloud Cottage), home for the Long Tom, a 4.7 inch veteran of the Boer War. They had enjoyed their gunnery practices, moving their big gun with horses borrowed from Tom Jones, who ran the Lynton to Minehead coaches. Now, though, the battles would not be mock ones and they had to say hurried goodbyes to their loved ones. Before the end of the year many of them would be at the Front Line.

Many more young men were needed to join the British Expeditionary Force in France. Lynton and Lynmouth played its full part in the recruitment drive, and many local men volunteered to fight for their country. Meanwhile the tourist trade slumped. The only influx of strangers was that of Belgian refugees. The following extracts from the columns of the *North Devon Journal* and *North Devon Herald* show how life changed at Lynton and Lynmouth in the months following the outbreak of war:

13 Aug. 1914. The Territorials had a hearty send off at Lynton on Saturday. Mustering at the Town Hall each man was presented by the

The Territorials mustering outside the Foresters' Hall (next to the Crown Hotel), 13 August 1914. War had broken out and they had been called up.

little Misses Legros with two packets of cigarettes and a cigar. Miss Riddell also thoughtfully gave each man a packet of stationery. Mr E.R.Hole, Chairman, Lynton Urban District Council, addressed the men, telling them to keep their hands steady and their gun muzzles straight. He assured them that during their absence their wives and families would be well looked after. As the men marched off to the station a big crowd gave them round after round of cheers.

13 Aug. 1914. Considerable public excitement was aroused by the arrest at Lynton on Tuesday of nine Germans, most of whom were waiters in the large hotels there. The prisoners were brought to Barnstaple by the last train. At Barnstaple Town Station a huge crowd gathered. At the Junction Station another crowd gathered, and a contingent of Territorials, armed with fixed bayonets, made a cordon around the prisoners until the Exeter train arrived.

The last line of defence: the Volunteer Training Corps outside the Town Hall, February 1916. Several men are wearing black armbands.

3 Sept. 1914. During the last week Lynton and Lynmouth have been in a state of ferment by reason of the fact that a number of German waiters are still being employed in hotels in the district, and also that Germans are resident here. Feeling has been growing, until it reached such a pitch that on Saturday night a large number of young men made a raid on one of the hotels where a German waiter was employed... Stones were thrown, and windows — purporting to be those of the sleeping apartment of the German — were smashed.

3 Sept. 1914. Probably the largest meeting ever held in Lynton was that which took place in the Town Hall on Monday evening. Every available corner was packed. The object of the meeting was to stimulate recruitment for Lord Kitchener's army and the other services... The chairman asked young fellows to bestir themselves and roll up. They would be fed, clothed, provided with pocket money, have no worries as to rates and taxes... Some twenty-two young men ascended the platform to

Painting by J. Vanderoost, a Belgian refugee, who lived in Lynmouth 1914-1915.

give their names for service, these being accommodated with seats on the plat-form.

3 Sept. 1914. We are sorry to state that very few visitors are coming into Lynton and Lynmouth. Though the excursions on the G.W.R. and the L.S.W.R. have been resumed, it has not made any difference to the twin villages. Steamer excursions have been few, and the motor charabanc service from Ilfracombe has been curtailed. Trade in every line of business is consequently very quiet.

10 Sept. 1914. The efforts to promote recruiting at Lynton have been attended with gratifying success. Young men to the number of about thirty have volunteered for some branch of the services. A batch of recruits, 24 strong, left Lynton on Saturday, for Lord Kitchener's army. Previous to their departure, Sir Thomas Hewitt addressed some words of encouragement to them from the Town Hall. Several thoughtful ladies supplied them with a good stock of cigarettes, matches, socks, chocolates and postcards, while Sir Thomas Hewitt gave each man half-a-crown.

10 Sept. 1914. The sum of £10 has been collected in the district to provide cigarettes for the Second Devons when they reach the fighting line.

10 Sept. 1914. A party from Belgium arrived at Lynton on Monday.

29 Oct. 1914. A meeting was held in the Lyn Valley Hotel to consider what steps could be taken to assist the Belgian refugees. It was decided to let houses at low prices that would just cover out-of-pocket expenses.

12 Nov. 1914. Sergeant Harris, of Lynton, in the First Devons, has received a kit bag, presented by Miss Halliday to the first Lynton man to be wounded at the front.

17 Dec. 1914. With a view to stimulating recruiting, a largely held

The unveiling of the War Memorial outside the Town Hall, December 1921.

meeting was held at the Town Hall on Saturday evening. Mr Tom Jones, who presided, said Lynton had already done well, having sent 191, while that day he had attested three or four more... Colonel Branston, who vigorously emphasised the need for more recruits, maintained that he had served for over forty years with the Colours, but at the outbreak of War he had at once offered his services in any capacity. He was still in hopes the authorities would find him something to do. Yet somebody at Lynton last week sent him a white feather!

31 Dec. 1914. Christmas in the twin villages was the quietest on record. Some of the lads in khaki paid a brief visit home and imparted a little cheer.

North Devon Journal, North Devon Herald, 1914

In a few short months life in Lynton and Lynmouth had changed dramatically. The war dragged on for another four years and in that time life was hard for those who remained at home. Yet their sacrifices were small compared with those who served overseas.

In December 1921 a war memorial was unveiled in front of the Town Hall. It listed the names of 41 Lyntonians who had given their lives for their country.

A German Bomber

ABOUT twenty-past seven on the morning of 24 July 1940, Lyntonians heard the roar of aircraft engines followed by the rat-a-tat-tat of rapid gunfire out over the Bristol Channel. Later the news spread that a German aircraft had been shot down on Martinhoe Common, three miles west of Lynton. Some locals rushed there to inspect the wreckage. Those who remained in town caught glimpses of the surviving members of the German aircrew when they were brought into Lynton to be held at the police station.

James Paterson in the cockpit, Reims aerodrome, France, May 1940.

The extracts which follow were written by one of the three Spitfire pilots responsible for shooting down the Junker Ju 88. Before giving his eyewitness account it would be helpful to provide some background information.

James Paterson was a New Zealander. In 1938 he qualified as a pilot with the Royal New Zealand Air Force and then sailed for England to serve with the RAF. When war broke out in September 1939, Paterson was only nineteen years old. He was sent to France, where he was an officer commanding a servicing flight and flew Magisters on reconnaissance patrols.

Life became much more eventful after the Germans invaded France in May 1940. In the weeks that followed the young man had more adventures and faced more dangers than most people do in a lifetime. In the air he flew on reconnaissance missions and carried vital despatches and supplies. On the ground he was in charge of large lorry convoys, which faced air attacks as they drove across war-torn France carrying desperately needed fuel, parts and ammunition for British squadrons.

Finally, on 17 June, with the French near to surrender, Paterson was ordered to evacuate his men. At the time his convoy was close to Brest so, abandoning vehicles and equipment, he and his men headed for the harbour. There at gunpoint he commandeered an old inshore ferry boat, crammed his 130 men on board and put to sea, less than twenty-four hours before the German Fifth Panzer Division captured the port. Two hours out, with fuel running low, they were picked up by a Belgian steamer which was loaded with troops, but even then they were not out of danger, for the vessel was attacked by three German dive-bombers. Fortunately the bombs just missed and the steamer reached Falmouth safely. Back in Britain James Paterson was trained to fly Spitfires and then joined 92 Squadron at Pembrey, South Wales.

Shooting Down the Ju 88

It was early on 24 July 1940 that the pilots of Red Wing, 92 Squadron, Pembrey were scrambled with orders to find and destroy an enemy aircraft which had been spotted over the Bristol Channel. Three Spitfires went up, piloted by James Paterson, John Bryson, a Canadian, and Brian Kingcombe, the Flight Commander. The following account of the shooting down of the German dive-bomber, and of a subsequent visit to Lynton, comes partly from Paterson's diary and partly from a letter he wrote a week later:

> **Diary:** This morning Red section were given a scramble. I was No 2. We intercepted a Ju 88 near Porthcawl at 12,000. He unloaded his bombs and dived like blazes. John Bryson went down after him firing short bursts, while Kingcombe and I took positions each side in order to keep sight of him when he went through cloud.
>
> **Letter:** Finally, after John had pumped off all he had, the Ju 88 turned in my direction and gave me a lovely deflection shot at him, making one of his engines stop and 'polishing off' his top gunner. He became easy meat then for a stern attack, so I gave him all the rest of my 2,600 rounds in many sharp dives from above and his starboard engine began to glow a bright red, and gave off a long stream of black smoke.
>
> We were almost at sea level by this time and the Jerry absolutely helpless, but the… coast loomed up all of a sudden and he had to make a sharp pull up to miss the cliffs. As he did this Bryne caught him a beauty

from a stern deflection setting the port tank on fire as well, making the thing go down across a moor and landing on its belly. We noticed someone jump by parachute just before the thing landed but too late, for although the 'chute opened he hit the deck before the strain was properly taken.

The dive-bomber finished up burning furiously with its nose through a stone fence and, as we circled round like hawks over their prey, it was a sorry sight to see one of the crew pulling two more wounded out of that flaming hell. After 'shooting' up the local village to make them 'turn out' to attend to the unfortunate devils and have a look at the parachutist, who we saw sit up and roll about once or twice, we 'tootled' home for breakfast.

Collecting Souvenirs

Later that morning the three pilots, together with their commanding officers, returned in Magisters and landed in a field beside the wreckage so that they could

The remains of the German dive-bomber on Martinhoe Common, 24 July 1940. James Paterson is cutting the swastika off the tail.

Photograph from the film found in the Leica camera showing German airmen at an airfield in France. The airfield was almost certainly the one the Junker Ju 88 had taken off from.

cut some swastikas and crosses from the smouldering fuselage, wings and tail. Much against orders Paterson also collected some other souvenirs:

Letter: My booty was a lovely little 50 guinea Leica camera, a Mauser .38 automatic, a German Mae West (they are miles better than ours) and the pilot's flying helmet (also better than mine). The film in the camera, I had developed later and it told a very interesting tale — including the aerodrome in France from which this machine came.

This photograph from the film shows German airmen being inspected.

A Visit to Lynton

Paterson then describes how he and his fellow pilots were taken to Lynton:

> **Diary:** We were taken to Lynton police station to see the crew.
>
> **Letter:** The local police took us to their lock up and showed us the prisoners, one of whom spoke English quite well. The pilot, an officer, was bruised in the back, the wireless operator had a sore head, the parachute guy was by this time dead and also the other gunner was fairly riddled like a sugar-shaker.
>
> **Diary:** The local hotel gave us free lunch and two fine bottles of Hock, after we had had many beers. A truly marvellous time was had by all.
>
> **Letter:** We were feeling fine when we finally took off again after signing dozens of autographs for the enthusiastic crowd which had arrived at the scene.

James Paterson was obviously elated when he wrote these accounts. It was hardly surprising, for this was the first enemy aircraft he had helped to shoot down.

Postscript

On 8 September Paterson was posted to Biggin Hill in Kent and took part in the later stages of the Battle of Britain. On the morning of 11 September he was involved in a dog fight with four Messerschmitt Bf 110s, destroying one and damaging others. That afternoon the tables were turned, for a Messerschmitt Bf 109 shot off half his wing and punctured his petrol tank. Flames engulfed the cockpit but Paterson managed to bale out. He landed safely, but was burnt around the eyes and was sent on leave to recuperate.

Pilots were desperately needed and on 25 September an eye specialist passed Paterson fit, though it seems he still had difficulty seeing properly. He returned to Biggin Hill to find that John Bryson and several other close friends had been killed in action. Two days later he was again shot down by enemy fighters. Other pilots saw the plane in flames and Paterson trying to struggle out of his cockpit. This time he failed and died in the crash. James Paterson was only twenty. After his death he was awarded an MBE for his outstanding services in France in 1940.

James Paterson cuts off a souvenir. The other two pilots who helped shoot down the Junker Ju 88 are with him; John Bryson on the left and Brian Kingcombe on the right.

Flo Hildick Remembers

There are still a few local people with memories of the day the German Ju 88 was shot down on Martinhoe Common. The account which follows was given to the author by Flo Hildick:

> I was twenty-nine at the time. I wasn't married then. My name was Flo Hodges and I was living with my three aunts in Queen Street, Lynton. Our family had a bakery which was called 'Hodges'. We had an old Austin 12 to take round the bread and my aunts bought me a little Austin 10 to drive round in.

It was still early. I've always got up early — you have to if you have a bakery — the men baked in the night and I had to get the shop ready before we opened. I think I was having a cup of tea when there was a terrific bang. Somehow I guessed a 'plane had crashed.

I called my cousin, Peter Goode. He was only nine. We didn't waste time. We jumped straight in our car and off we went. We went up the old Station Hill and drove in the direction the explosion had come from.

I don't think we passed a soul on the way. The roads were deserted. There was no one about. We parked the car near Woody Bay Station and began to run. I'm not sure how we knew where to look, I think perhaps we saw part of the plane sticking up. We ran across a field to one of those big hedges. Peter helped me scramble up the bank and then we slid down the other side.

We had the shock of our lives! There were Germans sitting there. They were wearing uniforms and had helmets on. They couldn't have been more than a few yards from us. They looked as surprised to see us as we were to see them. We sat down on the grass and looked at them. No one spoke, we just looked at each other. I didn't feel the least bit frightened. I'd always imagined Germans to be big fellows, but these seemed quite small. They didn't look as if they would do anyone any harm. They just looked so terribly sick.

There were three Germans, but I can only picture two of them. One sat slumped, with his head down and his back to the hedge. It is the other one I remember most. He was away from the hedge and he just sat there with his hands together, not moving. He looked at us as if he was not the least bit interested in what he saw. In fact in one way I felt sorry for them. They looked done in. Yet part of me said they were enemies and needed to be captured.

We were the first there. We were just beginning to wonder what to do when we heard the noise of a car. We weren't sure if we were really supposed to be there, so we decided to slip away.

We lingered nearby for a while. Lots of other people came streaming up. I'm not sure where they all came from. I remember speaking to a policeman and he said the Germans were all right.

Another photograph taken at the German-held airfield in France. James Paterson's notes indicate that the officer in the centre was the pilot of the aircraft shot down over Martinhoe Common.

Then we set off home. The road was busy by then. People must have been going out to see the crashed plane. 'Floss, I can't believe it!' Peter kept saying, all the way home. He was so excited.

Our family definitely didn't believe us when we got back and told them we had seen some Germans. We went in the bakery to tell the men. One said, 'You've been seeing things.' 'Yes, we have,' I said. Another said, 'Fancy that, Flossy going over the moor and seeing some Germans!'

Do you know, I've never told anyone about it since. But I can still see those Germans sitting there. It seems like a dream.

Flo Hildick's Memories as Told to the Author (1996)

Index

Albert Edward, Prince of Wales 68-70
Albion 125-26, 134
Appledore 34
Attree family 171-72

Bailey, Charles 18
Bailey, Charles (junior) 144, 149
Baker, Thomas 55, 70
bands 98, 124, 131, 134
Barnstaple 20, 33-34, 36, 49, 50, 55,
    58, 65, 68, 69, 87, 112, 113, 125,
    147, 149, 159
Barry 92, 156
Bath Hotel 56, 76, 77
bath-house 70-72
bathing 20, 23, 42-43
bathing machines 42-43
Belgian refugees 173, 176
Bevan, Cecil 44-48
Bevan, Mrs 65-66, 70
Bevan, Thomas 65, 75
Bevan, William 44, 55, 102, 104, 108
Bideford 59, 61, 112, 147
Blackmoor Gate 159-60
bowls 125-26
Bridgwater 51, 52, 166

Bristol 30, 59, 60, 64, 79, 87, 91, 146,
    156
building industry 99-111, 119-23, 136

Cardiff 64, 91, 156
carriages 22, 24, 26-28, 68, 69, 70, 136
Castle Hotel 28, 38, 52, 55, 56, 69,
    107-08, 114, 125
charges 62-63, 70-72
Cliff Railway 78, 81-82, 93-98, 104,
    105, 106, 108, 109, 120, 146-47
coaches 49-58, 112-18, 134, 138, 159,
    162-67, 173
Coleridge, Samuel Taylor 8-10
Colwill, Sam 56, 112-18
Colwill, Tom 117-18
Combe Martin 36, 113, 114, 160
Cooper, Dr Thomas 21, 37, 43, 49, 59
Cottage Hospital 116
Countisbury 24, 37, 47, 52, 54, 55, 65,
    67
Countisbury Hill 24-25, 28, 53
Crocombe, Jack 90-92
Crocombe, William 80-81
Crook, John 72, 104-06
Cross St 106

Crown Hotel 20, 49, 51, 108
cutting of the first sod 131-34

day-trippers 61, 108, 144, 152-57
Directions Hill 114-17
Dulverton 55, 56, 58

electricity 108, 109
enclosure 16-18
esplanade 77, 78, 85, 94, 105, 120, 147

ferns 43-44
floods 72-78
Foresters' Hall 174
Forrest Hall 90-92
Frederick William, Prince of Prussia 72
Fry, George 59

German bomber 179-86
Glen Hotel 136, 139
Glen Lyn 44, 115-16
Glenthorne 65, 66
Globe Inn 21, 35-36, 108
golf 136, 139
Groves, George 80-81
Groves, William 75

Halliday, Mr 65
harbour 29-31, 38, 59, 73-74, 75, 79-86, 87-91, 154
Hazlitt, William 8-10
Hewitt, Thomas 94, 96, 176
Hildick, Flo 184-86
Hodges, Lieutenant 88-89

Hollerday House 19-30, 134
Holman, John 55, 105, 129
Hooper, W. 36
hotels 20-23, 26, 27, 28, 56, 58, 61, 147-48, 183 (see also individual names)
Hunter's Inn 138, 140-42

Ilfracombe 11, 27, 33, 50, 51, 55-56, 58, 59, 60, 61, 66, 70, 112-18, 138, 159-60, 165
Island Cottage 65, 70

Jennings, Louis 105
Jeune, Mrs 96, 98
Jones, Bob 96, 98, 122
Jones Bros. 55, 96, 120-23
Jones's coach office 57, 58
Jones, Tom 125, 173

Kensington Boarding House 55, 56, 105, 107-08

Lake, Colonel Benjamin 135-51
Lee Abbey 18, 143-45
Lee Road 100, 120, 121, 162
lifeboat 88, 90-92
lime kilns 76
Litson, William 20-23
Little Jane 82, 84
Lock, John 25, 26
Lock, William, 16, 18
lodging-houses 20, 21, 23, 61, 139
Lyn Valley Hotel 44-46, 166, 176
Lynbridge 107-08, 124

Lyndale Bridge 27, 40
Lyndale Hotel 44, 54, 75, 102, 108, 155, 164
Lynrock Mineral-Water Company 168-72
Lynton Cottage 25, 153

manor 40, 73-74, 96, 102
manor house 99-100
Martinhoe Common 136, 138, 179, 180-81,184-86
Mary 81-83, 84, 86
Minehead 8, 11, 24, 50, 51, 52, 53, 54, 55, 56, 58, 90, 166
Moncrieff, A.R.H. 109
motor cars 158, 160
motor coaches 158-67, 176
Mundy, Revd Matthew 65

Nelson Cottage 76-77
New Inn 23
Newnes, Frank 127
Newnes, George 93-98, 108, 110, 119-27, 129, 131-34, 159-62
Newnes, Priscilla 119, 123-24, 126-27, 131-34

Parracombe 51, 69, 114
Paterson, James 179-83
Pedder, E.J. 76, 83, 84, 85-86, 106
pier schemes 94, 98, 99, 102-05, 108, 110, 120, 122, 152-57
piers 60, 137-38, 144-47, 149-51
poets 8-13
Porlock 33, 51, 52, 90, 91, 163

Portishead 60

railways 52, 53, 58, 60, 68, 69, 83, 84, 99, 102, 103, 113, 123, 131-34, 137, 139, 146-48, 152, 159-62, 166, 176
rectory 119
revel 35-37
Richards, Andrew 35-36
Rising Sun 76
roads 20, 24-28, 137-38
Roe family 18, 30, 73
royalty 68-72

sailing vessels 9, 75, 79-86, 87-89
St Mary the Virgin Church 35, 37, 38, 165
Sanford, William A. 25, 26
scenery 8, 9, 11, 12, 14-19, 20, 21, 22, 23, 62, 70
sea-fishing 26, 29-31, 44-48
Selwyn, Mrs 27
Shelley, Percy Bysshe 12-13
shipwrecks 79, 87-89
shooting 23, 38-40
Sillery Sands 42-43
smuggling 8, 32-34
South Molton 56
Southey, Robert 11, 14-15
standing stones 15-16, 18-19
steamers 59-64, 108, 117, 137, 144-47, 152-57, 176
students 40, 42
Summerhouse Hill 40-41
Summit Castle 119, 120, 125
Superb 87-89

Swansea 125-26
Swete, Revd John 15-16, 18

Taunton 51, 166
Territorial Army 173-74
Three Sisters 84-86
Thornton, Revd William 52, 65-67,
    70-72, 87-89
Topsy 80-81
Tors estate 99-104, 108
Tors Hotel 44, 100-03
Town Hall 124,173, 175, 177, 178
Trix, Mrs 70-72

Valley of Rocks 8, 9, 14-19, 23, 38, 39,
    173
Valley of Rocks Hotel 21-23, 28, 56,
    57, 72, 98, 104, 105, 108, 121, 134,
    160
Vellacott, Nathaniel 35
Vellacott, Richard 35

Wales 79, 83, 125
Warner, Revd Richard 24-25
Watersmeet 38, 166
Watty, William 80-81
Williams, T.H. 16, 18
Woody Bay 135-51
woollen industry 20
Wordsworth, William 8-10
World War One 173-78
wrestling 35-37
Wringcliff Bay 42-43